W9-BKO-534

Twayne's United States Authors Series

EDITOR OF THIS VOLUME

Sylvia E. Bowman

Indiana University

Horace Binney Wallace

TUSAS 287

HORACE BINNEY WALLACE

By GEORGE EGON HATVARY

St. John's University

TWAYNE PUBLISHERS

A DIVISION OF G. K. HALL & CO., BOSTON

Copyright © 1977 by G. K. Hall & Co.
All Rights Reserved
First Printing

Library of Congress Cataloging in Publication Data

Hatvary, George Egon.
  Horace Binney Wallace.

  (Twayne's United States authors series ; TUSAS 287)
  Bibliography: pp. 163 - 66
  Includes index.
  1.   Wallace, Horace Binney, 1817 - 1852—Criticism and inter-
pretation.
PS3129.W9Z7   813'.3   77-22984
ISBN 0-8057-7190-5

MANUFACTURED IN THE UNITED STATES OF AMERICA

S
3129
.W9
27

Contents

About the Author

George E. Hatvary received his Ph.D. from New York University, and he is at present an Associate Professor, formerly Chairman of the English Department, at St. John's University. He has published articles on Wallace and Poe in *American Literature, Princeton University Library Chronicle, Boston Public Library Quarterly,* and *Poe Studies.* He co-edited with T. O. Mabbott a facsimile edition of Poe's *Prose Romances* (St. John's University Press, 1968), and he is the editor of a forthcoming volume of Wallace's selected fiction in the *John Colet Archive of American Literature* series.

Preface

This work is the first full-length study of the writings of Horace Binney Wallace. Seldom has a writer of his caliber been so little known or so little remembered. This disservice to literature was Wallace's own doing. Novelist, critic, journalist, legal editor, philosopher, art historian, Wallace was morbidly secretive about all but his legal writings. Under one of his early pseudonyms, "William Landor," he was singled out for "high success" by Poe, who later unabashedly copied from his work; subsequently Rufus W. Griswold, maker of literary reputations, wanted to include him in the forthcoming *Prose Writers of America*, but Wallace refused all but a bare dedication. Griswold called his hard, persistent reticence "modesty," but in view of Wallace's suicide at the age of thirty-five, it is more illuminating to speak of self-destructiveness. Somewhere within him Wallace knew how much there was to destroy. The enormous signature on his extant letters stands as his privately recognized measure of his own gifts.

It is not my purpose here to claim for Wallace the rank of a Poe or an Emerson, but among American writers he certainly deserves a place. Author of the anonymous *Stanley* (1838), which was called "the most remarkable novel which has appeared in the century";[1] contributor to *Burton's, Graham's, Godey's, The Knickerbocker, The Home Journal,* and other magazines of the day; ghost writer for, and controversialist force behind, Griswold; shaper of American law; critical interpreter of Comte's positivism in America; commentator on Classical, medieval, and Renaissance art far ahead of his time, Wallace is worthy of study in his own right, as well as for the light he casts on two decades of American life and thought. It is an avowedly conservative, "Whiggish" light, as Perry Miller would put it, but one nonetheless focused sharply on such issues as the transition of American taste from Classicism to Romanticism, the rise of social and political egalitarianism, the status of art in America, to name but three. It is the light of a mind at once exalted by genius and tempered by a Classical bent—a highly cultivated, universal mind looming in relatively lonely eminence at a time when the idea of the Renaissance man was becoming increasingly rare, yet still a possibility.

Fortunately for us, John William Wallace collected some of his brother's writings in two posthumous volumes. These received glowing reviews, but they had to bear the unfair burden of establishing lasting literary fame in face of an almost total absence of Wallace's name from contemporary records. Still, one of them, *Literary Criticisms,* was reissued as recently as 1972![2] John Wallace's service to posterity was not matched by similar openness with regard to his brother's life. The first posthumous collection carried biographical material, but this was written by family members;[3] Wallace's suicide became public knowledge, for example, only by accident.[4] There is evidence that Wallace kept a diary, but it is not to be found, and the surviving correspondence is scant. We have John Wallace's statement that much of his brother's writings were yet to be collected,[5] but when years later he donated volumes of family papers to the Historical Society of Pennsylvania, nothing substantial pertaining to his brother—neither writings nor life records—was among them.[6]

Based on available material, Chapter 1 of this study sketches Wallace's life and secret literary career. Chapter 2 examines his earliest writings, which have appeared mainly anonymously or under pseudonyms. Since Poe knew many of these works and borrowed from them heavily, and since Poe's literary executor, Rufus W. Griswold, and Wallace were friends, Chapter 3 makes an attempt to throw some light on this still obscure but intriguing triple relationship. Chapter 4 glances at Wallace's legal writings and examines his articles and reviews, which appeared mostly in George P. Morris and N. P. Willis's *Home Journal.* Chapter 5 and 6 examine Wallace's writings during the last two and a half years of his life, which were collected in his posthumous *Art, Scenery and Philosophy in Europe.* Finally, Chapter 7 sums up Wallace's literary reputation beginning with the two posthumous collections to date.

I owe a debt of gratitude to the New York rare-book dealer J. J. Cohane, who many years ago called Wallace to my attention, noting a number of Poe's borrowings from him. Similarly, the late Thomas O. Mabbott noted Poe borrowings from Wallace and communicated these to me. During the initial stages of my research I received much kind help from Gay W. Allen and the late Nelson F. Adkins of New York University; Bertha Humez; Mme. Pierre Her-

Preface

vieux; and P. E. de Berredo Carneiro of the UNESCO and the Maison d'Auguste Comte in Paris.

I am grateful to several institutes for permitting me to publish excerpts from letters and other manuscript material in their collections. I am quoting such excerpts from Wallace material at the Historical Society of Pennsylvania, the Massachusetts Historical Society, the University of Virginia (Horace Binney Wallace Collection, Clifton Waller Barrett Library), and the Maison d'Auguste Comte; Griswold material in the Manuscripts and Archives Division of the New York Public Library (Astor, Lenox and Tilden Foundations) and in the Boston Public Library, by courtesy of the Trustees; and Wallace material in the Harvard College Library and Julia Ward Howe correspondence at the Houghton Library, both by permission of the Harvard College Library, the latter by personal permission also of John Richards. I wish to thank the above institutes further for extending their research facilities to me. Similar thanks are due to the Library of Congress, the Reference Division of the New York Public Library, the American Antiquarian Society, the New York Historical Society, the Brooklyn Public Library, and the libraries of the University of Chicago, New York University, St. John's University, Princeton University, and Columbia University.

I wish to thank the medical historians Peter H. Niebyl, M.D. and Jacques M. Quen, M.D. for expressing a psychiatric opinion about Wallace. I am grateful to Deborah Clifford for suggestions with reference to Julia Ward Howe. I wish, above all, to thank my wife Laurel for her critical readings of the manuscript and for the interest she has shared with me in Wallace.

GEORGE EGON HATVARY

New York, New York

Chronology

in five installments (1847 - 48); aids Griswold in his controversies leading up to the one involving Poe, in 1849 - 50.

1850 -
1851   Wallace spends a year in Europe; studies cathedrals, great paintings, and Alpine scenery. Forms a friendship with Julia Ward Howe in Rome; visits Auguste Comte in Paris and presents him with an annuity of 500 francs. Periods of nervous depression begin.

1852   Symptoms become more acute; Wallace embarks again for Europe in November; commits suicide by cutting his throat in Paris on December 16.

1855   John Wallace publishes his brother's last writings in *Art, Scenery and Philosophy in Europe*.

1856   Publishes *Literary Criticisms*.

1857   Publishes a second edition of *Art, Scenery and Philosophy in Europe* titled *Art and Scenery in Europe, With Other Papers*.

CHAPTER 1

Genius Bent on Self-Destruction

I   *The Family Mold*

H ORACE Binney Wallace was born on February 26, 1817, the
last child of a prominent, well-to-do Philadelphia family. Of
the three elder children, Susan was eleven, Mary seven, and John
two. Some years previously two boys had died in early childhood.
With the parents past forty, it is likely that Horace was more aware
of the burdens than of the advantages of being the youngest. In the
"Memoir," his brother John recalls his "dispositions" as
"somewhat individual and reclusive; never otherwise, however,
than as fond and amiable, and, when finely touched, as exhibiting
themselves in the finest issues of innocence and feeling."[1] The
passage suggests a sensitive child's refuge in solitude; we learn subsequently that Horace was particularly fond of nature. He seems to
have found companionship with John most easily, the respect of
the younger for the elder surviving into later life in the form of the
frequent whimsical address, "My Lord." The two brothers certainly remained close. As the last surviving members of their immediate family they were to live together and share an office, and
John was not to marry until six months after his younger bachelor
brother's death.[2]

The father, John Bradford Wallace, was a cultured man and an
able lawyer, but he was overshadowed by the maternal uncle and
godfather, Horace Binney, whose name the child was given. There
were also several illustrious forebears to admire and adopt as standards for subsequent conservatism and Federalist politics. There
was Grandfather Wallace, who had been a judge and a trustee of
Princeton College, and Great-grandfather Wallace, a prosperous
merchant of Scottish origin, who had entertained George
Washington on his New Jersey farm. Grandfather Binney, too, had
a revolutionary connection, having studied medicine with the great

Benjamin Rush and served as surgeon in Washington's army. More distantly, there were generations of interesting Bradfords going back to William Bradford, the famous Colonial printer who had helped young Benjamin Franklin establish himself in Philadelphia. In 1823, when John Bradford Wallace's vast land speculations west of the Alleghenies had brought him to the brink of financial ruin, he removed his family to the frontier town of Meadville, Pennsylvania, in order to supervise his business affairs and presumably to live more cheaply. The journey took three and a half days by stagecoach, and the shock of social and cultural isolation was severe, especially for the older members of the family. John B. Wallace did all that he could for his sons, whose education he took personally in hand, and for the town, which rewarded him by electing him to the State Legislature; he nevertheless appears in the subdued light of a man who failed. When after thirteen years of fruitless effort he returned to Philadelphia in 1836, he had lost a fortune and was broken in health and spirit and died early the next year.[3]

The mother presents a more enigmatic picture. Her brother, Horace Binney, speaks of her "uncommon faculties and virtues" and of her "uniformly bright and vivid" mind, but intimates that her trials—family deaths, including that of her eldest daughter, Susan, in 1842, in childbirth, the loss of family fortune, life in Meadville—set up anxieties in her that turned into a state of depression. In Binney's words, her spirit "never recovered what the world calls cheerfulness"[4]—a significant point in view of the depression that her son Horace was to suffer at the end of his life.

In the summer of 1826, Mrs. Wallace was planning one of her trips to the family seat of Burlington, New Jersey. Horace Binney wrote to her on August 24:

But is it to be temporary only? . . . Is Mr. Wallace's concern with that country such, that visits to it, of more or less length, will not suffice for his interests? Do you not contemplate some arrangement by which your children and yourself can be united under *your own* roof in this quarter of the country, among your friends and the friends of your children? If you do . . . I can at once provide you with a residence . . . one to be your own while you could use it, and that of your *daughters* in perpetuity, for we must let the *sons* rough it till the daughters are taken care of.[5]

Mrs. Wallace, who considered the environs of Meadville "signalized by the worst characteristics of democratic colonization,"[6] agreed to the family break. The boys remained in Meadville with their father, who, however, was also absent from time to time, presumably on business. There was much outdoor fun to be had on the edge of the wilderness, where "the track of the Indian was then scarcely obliterated, and the primeval forests still skirted the streets of the town"[7]—fishing and skating and sleighing—but no doubt also intermittent periods of loneliness and fear. There were frequent visits between Meadville and Burlington, but the fact remains that the boys were essentially deprived of their mother—John from his eleventh and the more vulnerable Horace from his ninth year on. He wrote to his father's sister before he was quite ten:

If Mama was here, we should have had a fine chance for mince pies; but as she was away, we had not any even at Christmas; for Priscilla [the servant] did not know how to make them. Nor did we have greens up at Christmas; Pa says that he can say as the boy did, he "has seen a hundred & a hundred Christmasses, but never such a one as this one." But still it was a pretty good one: Chriskingle brought us some sugar almonds and lemon candy &c the weather has been very cold indeed, & all the creeks are all frozen and there has been very good skating; & John & I have been skating a good many times.[8]

One suspects the boys were not entirely sheltered from the coarseness and violence of a frontier experience. If so, the Meadville years may well have reinforced that impulse of violence which was to run through some of Wallace's writings and gain final control over him.

If the mother's absence contributed to the brothers' closeness, Horace must have been made doubly lonely in the fall of 1829 when John left Meadville to attend the University of Pennsylvania, where Horace Binney was a trustee. "We have our eye upon my little namesake and Godson for a future occasion," Binney wrote to his sister;[9] accordingly, Horace followed John to Pennsylvania in the fall of 1830, before he was fourteen. His uncle wrote to his mother: "John and Horace are fixed in quarters & in College. The Provost told me this morning that Horace was well fitted, and was a great promise. He is much altered since I last saw him in Meadville, and every way for the better."[10]

An air of ambiguity surrounds the all-powerful, benevolent Horace Binney of the royal "we." He is remembered as one of the great lawyers of the age, who in 1844 defeated Daniel Webster in the famous Girard inheritance case before the U.S. Supreme Court. Appropriately, there is today a school in Philadelphia named after him. Among his contemporaries who paid tribute to his achievements, we find the lawyer and writer Sidney George Fisher, a member of the high society in which Binney moved. But Fisher, a sensitive and observant man, noticed another quality in Binney as well. He recorded in his recently published diary:

His character & talents are certainly very remarkable and his career has been eminently prosperous & successful. But he excites in me no strong admiration. He wants imagination, enthusiasm, soul. There is nothing in him allied to genius. His mind is clear, sound, acute, highly trained; his learning extensive and accurate; his character calm, firm, decided, prudent, cautious and cold. He wants impulsiveness, enlarged sympathies, quick feelings. He is haughty, distant, proud. He therefore excites no feeling in others. He is respected and admired, but not loved & he has no friends.[11]

The Wallace brothers were probably not unware of the ambiguous effects of their uncle's benevolence. The circumstances of their mother's departure from Meadville must have been clear to them, as was the surveillance under which they were being educated at the University of Pennsylvania. Horace formed an object of special interest to the distinguished man, who as his godfather and original bearer of his name "felt a sort of duty to observe him."[12] Horace Wallace reacted with much outward grace, but we can only surmise his corresponding feelings. In a letter he wrote at the age of twenty-eight to thank his uncle for some autographs, he made such a point of exalting the value of his uncle's signature over those he had enclosed that we cannot help questioning his sincerity.[13] Wallace, incidentally, lacked his uncle's impressive physical attributes. He was slight of build, with red hair, "not handsome," as Emily Chubbuck Judson was to note, with "nothing striking in his appearance."[14] Also he was shy. But he was no doubt conscious of possessing traits that Fisher missed in Horace Binney: impulsiveness, enlarged sympathies, quick feelings, or what we might call passionate imagination.

Adolescence seems to have accentuated the inner stresses. Some time after beginning his third year at Pennsylvania, where he was an outstanding student, especially in mathematics, Horace dropped out—as did, incidentally, a number of other students, displeased with the excessive authoritarianism of the school.[15] In a letter to his brother-in-law, on December 6, 1833, Horace Binney expresses willingness to have his nephew enter his office,[16] but whether Horace actually commenced such a short-cut course to law is uncertain, for that same winter he enrolled at Princeton to begin once again his junior year. He did splendidly. "His extraordinary attainments," writes a classmate, "were the wonder of all the college."[17] In mathematics his recitations assumed the quality of lectures. But he was solitary, gaining the reputation of someone "proud and aristocratic," and even the "Memoir," which tries to conceal the lost year, admits that he broke many of the college rules.

On graduation from Princeton in 1835—with lower honors than he "deserved, on account of his irregularities"[18]—he returned to the University of Pennsylvania to study medicine. But the physical aspects of the profession revolted him; so he turned to chemistry. Although he did outstanding theoretical work as Robert Hare's student, he abandoned chemistry also and came home to law, entering his father's office in 1836, then on the latter's death, the office of his uncle's partner, Charles Chauncey, Jr. He was admitted to the bar in 1840.

If these were years of indecision, they were also marked by the frustrating attempts of an intellect of cosmic aspirations to adapt itself to the confinement of a single discipline. Finally, it would appear, Wallace had had his experience with the sciences and was ready to move on toward the humanities, anticipating the hierarchy he was to admire so much in Comte's positivism. Law as a profession may have been a compromise—and perhaps a difficult one—in the process of his fitting himself into the family mold. But on a deeper level, since his college years, Wallace had been also pursuing his secret literary career.

His brother John was bound to play an important role in his choice of law. Leading the way through college with greater steadiness of purpose, if less conspicuous brilliance, John was a lawyer by 1836. Horace was clearly looking to him for guidance still; to be sure, there were important affinities between the two brothers. John Wallace was a man of cultivated tastes, with a love of art and books and a special interest in the art of printing. He was, like Horace, reserved, avoiding "general and promiscuous associations," and in politics there was certainly agreement between them, both being backward-glancing Federalists.[19] Writing to Richard Henry Dana, Sr. after his brother's death, John Wallace noted that "there was scarcely any matter . . . when a common action was ever required, in which either was not sure to act for both in the way in which each would have acted for himself. And our estimates & judgments of men & character were almost identical."[20]

It is not surprising therefore that Horace should follow John in his professional life. John himself had shied away from the courtroom, preferring legal scholarship, which would bear such fruit as his noted history of court reporting called *Reporters* (1844) and eventually lead him to serve with dubious success as reporter to the U.S. Supreme Court.[21] Horace, sharing offices with him, entered into collaboration with John Innes Clark Hare to produce a long series of legal editions—somewhat against his deeper inclinations. It was Hare himself, his friend and intimate associate, who expressed his regret that Wallace had not practiced law, "for unlike most men of books his powers were greater for action than for speculation; and so close, precise and accurate was his mind that his advice was invaluable in business transactions, and his opinion of a title better than that of most men who pass their lives in reading abstracts."[22] We shall see further signs in Wallace of this propensity for action, which was to a large extent repressed until its final violent reign. As for his own attitude toward the law, he could write enthusiastically about it, hailing the beauties especially of equity. But he could also admit in private correspondence that a particular law book in progress was "very tedious."[23]

For the brothers were ultimately far more different than might appear. As a counterpart to the creative fires burning in Horace, John had only a "genial and humorous vein"[24] to offer. Horace was the troubled genius who reached for the stars and was blasted; John lived out a long, quiet, conventional life.

II *Man of Letters in Incognito*

By the time Wallace graduated from Princeton he was deep in writing. The "Memoir" gives the year 1834 as the beginning of his professional authorship; certainly by 1835 his first pieces had begun to appear in George P. Morris's *New York Mirror*, probably anonymously at first, then under the pseudonym "William S. Somner."[25] Wallace returned to anonymity with "The Authorship of the Doctor," a learned article published in the *Knickerbocker Magazine*, demonstrating that *The Doctor* was written by Robert Southey.[26] Another early piece, not published separately but later incorporated into *Stanley*, shows the rebellious direction of much of young Wallace's thinking. After introducing Henry St. John, Viscount Bolingbroke, dedicatee of Pope's "Essay on Man," as a man who "kept Miss Gumley, the most expensive prostitute in the kingdom," and once in a fit of drunkenness had run naked through the town and denied miracles, revelation, and the immortality of the soul, Wallace goes on to say,

I am amazed at the neglect into which the writings of this great philosopher have fallen. . . . He is the only infidel derider of man, from whose writings you come exalted, ennobled. . . . He looked on man with the scowl of a demon, and on truth with the smile of a seraph. His intellect was brilliant, though disordered; splendid, though erring; bright, but blasted. The gorgeous structure of his philosophy is riven to the foundation; but genius always commends our sympathy, for, "like the temples of the gods, she is venerable even in ruins."[27]

Wallace's attraction to the denying intellect ran deeper than a mere literary device. Four years later, after a visit to the Channings in Newport, Rhode Island, he was to write to his brother, disparaging both William Ellery Channing, Sr. and his Unitarianism:

The Dr. is quite unendurable. A Christian without the respectability of religion, an infidel without the bold attractiveness of denial. This weak, unconscious, obligatory scepticism, which is Christianity refused and Atheism not affirmed is wearisome and offensive. The attempt to make religion poetry, has ended in making poetry religion. It is laughable to see a man calling out his family and guests to perform an act of worship by gazing on the moon, the clouds and silent trees. If the Dr had more intellect he would be an infidel.[28]

Considering the rigors of Wallace's legal studies, one can appreciate all the more the forcefulness of the literary impulse that made 1838 the *annus mirabilis* of his youth. In this year *Stanley* saw light, another novel, *Henry Pulteney*, began to be serialized in *Burton's Gentleman's Magazine*, and a short story and two essays appeared in the same publication and in *Godey's Lady's Book*. Wallace was now using the pseudonym "William Landor," but with a characteristically offhand attitude, "Landor" becoming sometimes a mere "L." Later Wallace would reach for the name "John H. Meredith" or initials such as "J.H.M." or "J.K." or

"R.B." without any apparent consistency or significance. He certainly gives the impression of someone trying to escape, rather than to establish, a single pseudonymous identity. When *Stanley* appeared toward the end of 1838, the title page carried no author's name.

But the authorship was known to some. Edgar Allan Poe, for example, who as co-editor with William Burton of the *Gentleman's Magazine*, then editor of *Graham's Magazine*, bought pieces from "Landor," knew him to be the author of *Stanley*. Writing to "William Landor" in the summer of 1841,[29] he makes an indirect reference through Bolingbroke to *Stanley;* then later that year he says publicly, in "A Chapter on Autography,"

Mr. Landor acquired much reputation as the author of "Stanley," a work which was warmly commended by the press through the country. He has also written many excellent papers for the Magazines. . . . He is an elaborately careful, stiff, and pedantic writer, with much affectation and great talent. Should he devote himself ultimately to letters, he cannot fail of high success.[30]

Whether Poe ever made the association between "Landor" and Wallace is as uncertain as whether the two men ever met. But their possible lack of personal acquaintance did not preclude a curious literary relationship between them, as will appear.

Rufus Wilmot Griswold, the noted anthologist and Poe's subsequent literary executor, made the discovery of "William Landor's" identity sometime between 1842 and 1845, while collecting material for his forthcoming *Prose Writers of America*. Although Wallace refused to be included in the work, a friendship and literary association sprang up between the two men which was to become useful to them both. It is already in this context that Griswold attempted his dedication: "To / Horace Binney Wallace / of Philadelphia / Whose Abilities, Learning and Honorable Character / Give Assurance That / The New Generation / Will Prove Itself not Inferior to the Old / This Volume / Since his Modesty in Publishing his Writings Anonymously has / Prevented me from Testifying in Another Part of it / My Estimation of his Merits, / Is Very Respectfully Inscribed."[31] Yet, since *The Prose Writers of America* appeared only in the spring of 1847, it is surprising to read in the "Memoir" that the types were already set when Wallace asked Griswold to reduce the dedication to a mere mention of his name. It is less likely that Wallace changed his mind at the last minute than that Griswold had gone ahead somewhat insensitively on his own intrying to make his friend famous.

We shall have more to say about Griswold. Here it will suffice to note that both the friendship and the literary association were a complement of opposites. Griswold, an essentially superficial man but one highly skilled as an editor and publicist and endowed with personal attractiveness and charm, became for the rest of Wallace's life his most important contact with the literary world. Wallace never hesitated to call on Griswold to help him in what seemed to him a worthy cause, whether it was making R. H. Dana, Sr.'s lecture series on Shakespeare a success, or encouraging some young, unestablished writer. In exchange, Wallace wrote long, favorable reviews of Griswold's anthologies, supplied him with advice, even ammunition, in his various controversies, and wrote works on Washington and Napoleon which were eventually to be connected with Griswold's name. It is no great exaggeration to say that in place of the "Landor" mask which had worn thin by 1845, Wallace had found another—Rufus W. Griswold.

With the extinction and eventual burial of "William Landor" went also Wallace's fiction and his more belletristic non-fiction. Sometime probably in 1843, reaching impulsively for the long-discarded "William S. Somner," Wallace addressed a letter to the publisher Isaac Lea, speaking of a book of architecture by a "Mr. Somner of Princeton, N.J.," which he, Wallace, was ready to submit for examination;[32] and in 1844 "William S. Somner" himself addressed a letter to John Allen, editor of the *Knickerbocker Magazine*, identifying himself as the author of "The Authorship of the Doctor" and offering to write further articles on Southey.[33] Nothing seems to have come of these projects; we do not even know whether these letters were ever sent.

Whether we can detect in this shuffling of plans and masks the shadow of self-annihilation which was to engulf Wallace in seven years is a matter for interpretation. But there is a kind of cry in the night coming from him at this time in his "Monologues among the Mountains":

Once more, back to the life of the Mind!—to the spring and flash of Thought, and the boundless sweep of the Feelings! In the atmosphere of the world I can no longer get my breath; in its keenest enterprises I live but half my being: but, here, amid the solitudes of the mountains and sky, I once more feel my soul within me.[34]

St. Peter's College Library
St. Peter's College, Jersey City, N.J. 07306

The first of the "Monologues" as it appeared in *Graham's Magazine* rose to a climactic passage of inner frustration that was understandably suppressed, presumably by John Wallace, in the version reprinted in *Literary Criticisms:*

There is within me a power that would wreak itself upon creation; but the remorseless, insatiable brood of snake-like cares stiffen out their endless length of necks to suck from the heart of man its strength and inspiration; and the wolf-soul, chained by custom, must moan when it ought to crash through the forest, and must churn between its teeth its foaming rage and slap the air with the scarlet pulses of its restless tongue.[35]

Scarcely less revealing is the elaborate guise Wallace creates for the delivery of these extended "Monologues." Their author is "A Cosmopolite," characterized over four closely-printed pages as an extraordinary genius, over six feet tall, "with a countenance of antique and almost royal dignity." Like the villain Tyler in *Stanley,* the Cosmopolite has been everywhere and done everything "wild and romantic to the last degree," only he is benevolent. He is now old, "showing the fatigues rather than the fires of passion"; he dreams, in fact, of saving human time by being born old, "yet with the recollection of a past to look back upon . . . just as the world, (we must suppose, to reconcile Scripture with geology,) was created with all the formations that belong to an advanced stage of its existence."[36]

But the creation of the Cosmopolite was hardly an efficient mask vis-à-vis the editor who had originally requested copy from Wallace. In an accompanying note Wallace felt the need to adopt a contemptuous tone toward his "Monologues": "I have *whirled* you off some rhapsodies which you can kick into sense or lick into shape. . . . No thanks for them; for such things I can write by the foot, yard, perch, mile, or if necessary even by the league." But the beginning of the note belies its tone: "I have been overrun, my dear Henry, by ten thousand armies of occupation ever since I received your request; engaged daily at my office from nine in the morning till ten at night; investigating some important trust titles, and with other engrossing concerns. They have left me little time and no eye-sight.[37] And the cry resounds, breaking through the elaborate Cosmopolite mask: "Above all things—FREEDOM."

Wallace's middle period includes a large volume of editorial articles and book and drama reviews. His chief outlet for these was

George P. Morris's *National Press* (later, with N. P. Willis's co-editorship, called *Home Journal*), established in February, 1846. Wallace's friendship with Morris seems to date back at least to the *New York Mirror* days, and Wallace wanted to help the new publication, as he had helped Morris during the financially difficult winter of 1844 - 45 by writing about him and his songs.[38] Possibly, although Wallace was scrupulous in demanding pay for his work from editors, he sent Morris copy gratis, at least until the *National Press* was well on its feet.[39] In any case, when we consider Wallace's cluster of motives—to help an editor friend, to play the conservative but always patriotic gadfly to society, to plead the cause of a worthy author—we see a remarkable benevolence shining through.

"I know how ready you are, dear Horace, to do honor to the genius of American youth, and to advance the interests of un-friended worth wherever found," wrote George P. Morris in 1847, enclosing a book by James D. Nourse of Kentucky for Wallace to review.[40] But Wallace helped not only young writers. A letter in behalf of a member of the Shippen family seeking admission to Princeton,[41] another addressed to the then Senator James Buchanan in behalf of an impoverished friend seeking employment,[42] one recommending Robert Hare, his former professor of chemistry and father of J. I. Clark Hare, for the presidency of the American Philosophical Society,[43] several letters in service of the success of Dana's Shakespeare lectures[44] survive as examples on all levels. J. I. Clark Hare, writing to the younger Dana after the "irreparable" loss to him caused by Wallace's death, also speaks of "the powers which he was more ready to use for the benefit of others than for his own."[45]

But, as many also noted, Wallace presented an exterior of coldness. "His face was sharp and of a saturnine expression," wrote Parke Godwin, "and his manners were cold, until intimacy had broken through the outer wall of reserve, when he became frank, cordial, and communicative."[46] Horace Binney called this quality the initial shyness of a sensitive person, denying Wallace's "reserve."[47] J. I. Clark Hare, who knew Wallace perhaps better than did anyone, speaks in the same vein but more analytically: "He was so little understood, that most men called him cold and indifferent; mistaking the restraint of will and habit for insensibility of temperament and ignorant of the ardent feelings which lay hid beneath that calm exterior. Yet altho' all the emotions and

passions which form the exterior wrapping of the soul were in him
strong and vehement the soul itself was almost feminine in purity
and gentleness."[48]

We need not accept Hare's precise geography of psychic layers.
Passion, sensitivity, coldness—a Binney trait?—emerge from other
evidence also as important ingredients in Wallace's inner conflict.
His own brother spoke of "his sympathies with general society" as
"few and irresponsive."[49] Hare goes on to say, "As a friend he had
but one fault that he never asked, and would seldom receive the
aid of his friends, but his whole heart, and his whole strength were
always at their service."[50] How can we account for such extreme,
insistent self-reliance on the reverse side of the coin of
benevolence?

Wallace was certainly a man of masks, and we may turn Hare's
analysis around and ask whether Wallace's need to do good might
not be a conscious, even guilty, answer to a recognition of coldness
within himself. For, as Hawthorne never tires of showing in his fiction, masks are perilous, implying something more aggressive than
mere secrecy. How else can we explain that teasing, contemptuous
holding back of a part of the self from view—the need to see
without being seen? The world is simply not deserving of the
bestowal of the total self. Given the need to write, anonymity
becomes the best solution. Ah, but at what price! The mask grows
onto the face, and two or more selves split further and further.

The same self-destructive strain may well be the clue to
Wallace's enigmatic relationship to women. We have relatively little to go on in this area—two interesting friendships and one or two
glimpses besides. That Wallace had a great respect for intellectual
achievement in women is clear from both his published writings
and his correspondence. It is safe to assume that his mother and
possibly his sisters had an influence on his high standards in this
regard. He writes about Channing's daughter Mary in the same
letter we noted above:

Our friend Miss C. does not prove upon further acquaintance, so agreeable
a person as the little that I saw of her in Philadelphia would have led me to
suppose. You do not find in her conversation a portion of the bold flash or
subtle fire of another of our nearer acquaintance. She has fine feelings, &
more intelligence than intellect. Her mind does not present the firm &
springing re-action to that of her companion which is necessary to very interesting conversation. She is very soft & good as a woman should be; but
her simplicity sometimes passes into simpleness.[51]

That Wallace had an eye for beauty in women emerges here and there in his writings. In addition, in a playful letter addressed to a young cousin in 1845 he bemoans his loss of a "lady 'throned by the west' " in rivalry with a Dr. Gerhard, writing, "Will you not pity me?—or will you rather, unkindly, mock at my calamity?"[52] But of Wallace's total response to women we remain ignorant. All that we can grasp is an indistinct pattern of reticence.

Wallace's friendship with Emily Chubbuck, who wrote under the name "Fanny Forester" and was one of the first advocates of higher education for women, is illustrative. She and Wallace met sometime in 1845 in Philadelphia, where she had gone for her health, and they were in some ways impressed with each other. She wrote of him:

He is a man of talent, a scholar, and a perfect gentleman; refined, high-bred, delicate, and manly. He is not handsome; that is, there is nothing striking in his appearance; but he has a very intellectual look, and a peculiarly sweet expression. He is about as large as—; has an easy, gentlemanly carriage, and never does anything awkward. . . . He is an excellent critic, not only of books, but of painting, sculpture, etc. His conversation is more improving and interesting (combining the two beautifully) than any man's I ever met.[53]

Wallace invited her to a ball, writing to Griswold on December 3: "I have spoken to my sister, Mrs. Riddle, who promises me that she will go to the ball to-morrow, & will *matronize* the Forester. . . . I hope you will bring your influence, (which I have cause to think great) to bear in favor of Miss Forester's accompanying us."[54] But the aloofness beneath the playful tone is evident. Emily Chubbuck must have noticed the same quality in Wallace's manner, and shifted her original enthusiasm about him accordingly. No doubt, Wallace was not a serious obstacle when later that month she met the ardent Baptist missionary, Adoniram Judson—a man twice her age and recently bereft by the loss of his second wife—and fell in love with him.

Wallace meanwhile turned the relationship into chivalric friendship. On January 1, 1846, he visited Emily Chubbuck, and when she showed him—laughingly—an unfavorable review of her *Trippings in Author-Land* in the *Gospel Messenger*, he became indignant, writing later in his diary: "If I can find any proper place I will cuff this reverent booby over the mazard, in the way that his insolent coarseness deserves."[55] This is incidentally Wallace's one recorded outburst of anger. Whether he ever chastised the reviewer of the *Gospel Messenger* we do not know; but he did write a glowing review of *Trippings in Author-Land,* which appeared on February 21 in the *National Press.* And during Emily Chubbuck's romance with Judson he stood courteously by—if "alarmed" at the prospect of her going to Burma. "What induced you to suspect that I was going to Burmah?" she wrote to him on February 23, after having left Philadelphia for New York in a state of sudden illness which had prevented her from seeing him for "a good, cozy, confidential talk."[56] Wallace replied on March 1: "From the moment in which I first heard the name of this eminent and honored person pronounced by your lips, I saw and predicted the result."[57] The rest of the letter is written in the same vein of overcourtly solicitude, as though the writer were trying to hide something—perhaps his initial inability to respond fully to the lady. The Judsons were married in June and sailed in July from Boston. Since Wallace had promised to see Emily Chubbuck Judson off, they probably had their "good, cozy, confidential talk" to help her through the ordeal of uprooting herself, which loving the great missionary had cost her.

Another interesting question pertains to Poe's death, which took place in October, 1849. Griswold is chiefly remembered today as Poe's literary executor, who maligned Poe's memory in an obituary signed "Ludwig" and subsequently altered some of Poe's letters to put himself in a more favorable light in his relationship with the dead poet. Since the records show Wallace to have been a scrupulously just and honorable man, the question arises how we can reconcile his friendship with Griswold in the light of such evidence. In all probability Wallace was unaware of the altered letters, though it is safe to guess that if he had been aware he would have probably scolded his excessively publicity-minded friend, then forgiven him. As for Wallace's attitude toward Poe, the question is so intricate and intertwined with the literary relationship between the two men that it is best reserved for a later chapter. Here let us simply note that it is hardly to be expected that any contemporary from whom Poe had been plagiarizing for years would have much love for him in return.

Wallace, in fact, added fire to the controversy that began to rage over the "Ludwig" obituary, writing, "What a profound, complete and exquisite estimate of the character of Poe!" More subtly and more damningly he argued that in asking Griswold to be his literary executor Poe had "felt assured" that Griswold "would do in the best manner what probably no other would do at all."[58]

And writing to Griswold on May 4, 1850, he offered to review the "Ludwig" article and some of those attacking it "in a distant and impartial way." But Griswold would have to supply him with all the pertinent material immediately, for he was on his way to Europe, his brother having already sailed.[59] Perhaps Griswold never did. Unfortunately for a deeper understanding of Wallace's attitude toward Poe, no such article is to be found.

III   *Suicide*

During his European tour of 1850 - 51 Wallace probably saw relatively little of his brother. John Wallace was traveling as a representative of the Law Association of Philadelphia, and much of his time was spent visiting legal institutions and distinguished barristers in England and Scotland. Horace had gone abroad primarily to study great art, with the result that his ideas on aesthetics would be the best remembered aspects of his work. If during the years between 1845 and 1850 he had let his literary interests dwindle somewhat into journalism, now in his brief final period, although he could not or would not return to fiction, he had found a mode of doing justice to his deeper thoughts and perceptions. It is revealing of his own mental attitude that he was able for the first time in his life to state his vocation publicly as "literary and art critic."[60]

Yet the great flight had its ominous aspects. Many of Wallace's observations during his travels through the British Isles, France, Germany, Switzerland, and Italy reveal his growing interest in death. Of the remains of the thirteenth-century abbey at Netley, he writes: "Ruin seemed to have invested itself in its most enchanting traits . . . and I knew not whether most to mourn the structure which once was so peerless, or to love the destruction which had made it yet more captivating in overthrow."[61] The snowy silence on the Simplon Road moves him to record: "Even the last social, guarding, redeeming influence seemed extinct in the glittering beauty of death" (*ASE*, 175).

Wallace reached Rome in December. Here, at a Christmas party given by the American sculptor Thomas Crawford and his wife Louisa, Wallace met for the second time Crawford's sister-in-law, Julia Ward Howe. Their first meeting had taken place sometime

previously in Philadelphia, at which time Wallace had angered
Mrs. Howe, as she writes in her *Reminiscences* fifty years later, "by
his ridicule of Boston society, of which he really knew little or
nothing. He was now in a less aggressive frame of mind, and this
second meeting with him was the beginning of a much-valued
friendship."[62]

Julia Howe was living in Rome with her two small children, her
husband having returned to America earlier. She and Wallace saw
each other frequently, and as she was working on her first book of
poems, she not only found Wallace's criticism invaluable but believed that he would be able to make "all necessary arrangements"
for its publication.[63] In her *Reminiscences* she writes of Wallace as
an "exhilerating companion" with a "silvery *timbre*" to his rather
high voice. They visited historic sights together and had much
merriment over their both having red hair. "I was much pleased to
learn from him that 'the highest effort of nature is to produce a
rosso'" (pp. 198 - 99).

Julia Howe was an attractive young woman with much charm,
vivacity, and above all, ambition; but she was beset by intellectual
uncertainties. Her considerably older husband, the philanthropist
Samuel G. Howe, could provide little aid in this direction; he was
in fact resentful when in her frequent states of loneliness—which,
she admitted guiltily, her children were powerless to alleviate—she
sought the intellectual support she needed from others.[64] Wallace,
who introduced her to the writings of Auguste Comte and was able
to bring forth her "best thoughts,"[65] came to mean much to her.
There is little doubt that their friendship answered a need in her
deep enough to assume the character of love; nor is it surprising
that Wallace was able to give her all she wanted from him. His role
seems—perhaps simply because of the absence of any letters from
him to her—more passive. What we know of him would certainly
support the impression inherent in her calling him in her most exalted moments "my brother."[66]

In January Wallace went south to Naples. He rode on horseback
to the base of Vesuvius, from where he made the ascent on
foot—rejecting the guide's "machinery of ropes and sticks.
. . . Nothing but the roughness of the lava surface, and its softness,
which enable you to anchor your legs knee deep in the soil, renders
the ascent practicable. A series of vehement rushings brought me at
length to the top." From there he looked down into what was, since

last year's eruption, "a still raw and open ulcer of earth." He saw "knob-like blossoms of brilliant white, yellow, green, red, brown—the sulphurous flowers of Hell. . . . It was like Death. . . . It seemed the emblem of destruction, itself, extinct. There was something about it revoltingly beautiful, disgustingly splendid" (*ASE*, 193).

He probably crossed the Adriatic to Greece, going as far as Constantinople, as he had planned. By March he was back in Rome, and by April in Paris, where on the twenty-second he paid his first visit to Auguste Comte, living alone in "respectable" poverty in the rue Monsieur-le-Prince. Besides being a reader of the exciting new positive philosophy, Wallace was clearly aware of aspects of Comte's life, which had appeared in the sixth volume of the *Cours de philosophie positive*, in 1842. There Comte had spoken of his "temporary insanity" and attempted suicide, so that it is safe to suppose that the pull he exerted on Wallace was both intellectual and emotional.[67] Comte, whom Wallace describes as "considerably below my height, but with broad shoulders and a manly, full presence," dressed in black, and "highly nervous," with twitching hands and face, welcomed him warmly and talked brilliantly and wittily and almost uninterruptedly for two hours.[68] Wallace records with great interest Comte's thoroughgoing political conservatism. Comte, a supporter of Louis Napoleon's coup which would make him Emperor at the end of the year, told Wallace, "The doctrine of equality is an absurd and mischievous falsehood. . . . Rights of man—I deny that man has any rights: he has duties only." We can surmise from Wallace's subsequent letter to Comte from America that Comte spoke also of his rejection of Christianity in favor of his Religion of Humanity, which he was working out at this time; but instead of the sharp disagreement that Wallace was to express later, he probably merely listened to this renewed echo of the "bold denial" which had fascinated him since youth. On a personal level Comte probably mentioned his unhappy marriage, certainly his great chaste love for Clotilde de Vaux now dead for the past five years, for he referred to his apartment as one "consecrated to me by souvenirs of the most touching kind." Finally, whether during this visit or a subsequent one, Comte mentioned the "sacredotal subsidy" which his disciple Émile Littré had organized for his support; for before leaving Paris Wallace made a pledge of an annuity of five hundred francs to

Comte in recognition of his "contribution to the truth," earning for himself not only Comte's lifelong gratitude but also Comte's designation of him as his foremost American disciple.[69]

By May, Wallace was in London, where the International Exhibit had just opened. Almost a daily visitor to the famous Crystal Palace, he wrote enthusiastically to the *Home Journal* about this great show of materialistic progress. Later that month he returned to America—with every intention of going to Europe again, perhaps for a more extended stay than a year.[70] Europe was certainly in his system. On a hot August day he wrote to his brother, who had gone to Newport, "The small remains of me, not already mingled with the air in an evaporated form, will set off this morning for New York, hoping to pull up in the surf of Rockaway with the evening. I put the handbook of Central Italy in the bag, to make myself believe I am going to Rome."[71]

Otherwise, "all is going on well," Wallace continues. William, their office boy, and Jemmy their manservant, are "angelically perfect as usual." The dog Spring died, but "was interred in the end of the garden with funereal pomps—& William made an affecting elegy on the subject." The letter heightens the picture John Wallace was later to draw, for the elder Dana, of his and his brother's living in the civilized comfort of their house on Portico Square in perfect harmony.[72]

John Wallace's sorrowful letter is the source also of his brother's final symptoms. The periods of depression noted by Julia Ward Howe continued. Wallace complained of failing eyesight and of insomnia. His sister Mary's death in May, 1852, under "distressing circumstances" particularly affected him. He was apparently closer to her than was John, for he alone went to Louisville, Kentucky, to watch her die. Having lost their sister Susan in 1842 and their mother in 1849, the two brothers were now alone. Horace returned from the long journey in a state of physical and emotional exhaustion. In September he made an abrupt departure from home without leaving a note for John, as was his habit, as to his whereabouts. "When he came home he told me that his 'eyes had completely broken down' 'that a smash had taken place': 'that he had been *running about because he could not stay still.*' " They consulted physicians, among them the distinguished William Horner, one of whose visits induced a change in the patient from "a gloomy state of spirits" to "bouncing spirits." Horner saw nothing wrong with him except "a functional derangement of his nervous system" and advised a change of scene.

Accordingly, Wallace went to New York, booked passage for a voyage to Europe, then returned to Philadelphia. His brother writes: "He . . . came into my office, set himself down at my table & with great composure told me that he was very unwell, & thought that he was going to die. 'You need not be alarmed,' he said, 'I am not afraid to die; but I am afraid that I shall first loose [sic] my mind. I have no fear that I shall do anything violent; but I fear I shall sink into a state of imbecility or inertia.' " He added that he was "distinctly conscious, he thought, of failure of his memory."

The physicians' assurances continued. One admitted the possibility of "congestion of certain optic vessels at the base of the brain," but an oculist among them said that "nothing was the matter with his eyes at all." Visual problems were, incidentally, common in the nineteenth century among those who read much, so that if Wallace was looking for a hysterical symptom he did not have to look far. Among those close to him, not only Julia Ward Howe complained of poor eyesight, in the letter we shall see, but also his brother John.[73]

John accompanied him to New York, where yet another "eminent physician, a friend of his own," assured him that there was "nothing important" the matter with him except "too much blood on the brain," for which the voyage was "exactly the thing." His brother would wind up his affairs and follow him later, and on November 13 Wallace embarked on the *Arctic*.

On board ship he met William Cullen Bryant, whom he might have known previously, since Bryant was a friend of the Danas. Interestingly, Bryant has been described somewhat similarly to Wallace as gentle in manner but cold; Parke Godwin even applied the same term, "saturnine" to them.[74] At any rate, the two men seem to have found a common ground, notwithstanding their differences of political opinion. Wallace later wrote that he had found in Bryant's conversation his "chief stay and support."[75]

From Liverpool Wallace went to London, where he delivered documentary proof to the genealogist John Bernard Burke of the Philadelphia Wallaces' descent from Scottish royalty. It is tempting to see this act as a preparation for death, but John Wallace was at least as anxious to establish his royal descent as was Horace; he may even have been the motivating force in their common pursuit.[76]

Wallace reached Paris in a state of depression. He took lodgings at the Bains de Tivoli, a hydrotherapeutic establishment, and placed himself under the care of Dr. Bertin, a specialist in nervous ailments. On December 8 he wrote to his brother: "I am sorry to be able to give you but a bad report of my health. My exhaustion has been greater since I have been in Paris than at any previous time. . . . I hope and fight on still."[77] On December 13 he went to see Comte, who later referred to "the sacred visit of the eminent American, whose approaching decease I was far from dreading, notwithstanding the sad tone of his farewell."[78]

On the same day Wallace wrote to his brother, "Dr. Bertin, at my request, wrote to you . . . that your coming out would be important to me. I believe the chief matter is that I am exceedingly nervous. . . . I should certainly find your company a great satisfaction. . . . I have sometimes been in the deepest depression and alarm, and at other times am a little better. Travelling agitates and fatigues me, and repose alone brings depression. . . . Come if conveniently you can."[79]

Three days later Wallace cut his throat.[80] The frenzied violence implied by this mode of suicide suggests a state of psychosis; Wallace's lucidity just three days previously, his physicians' inability to find any organic disturbance, and his fluctuations between "bouncing spirits" and depression would suggest a manic-depressive or agitated-depressive state.[81] The "insanity" he himself had feared for some time was thus in a sense fulfilled. "I have no fear that I shall do anything violent," he had assured his brother perhaps in order to suppress the rumblings of violence within. "His reason had been overthrown," wrote his brother to the elder Dana.[82]

It is worth noting in this connection that Wallace's maternal aunt, Mary Binney Sargent, who died at the age of thirty-eight, was "afflicted with a clouded mind, the latter years of her life,"[83] and that his mother's spirit, according to Horace Binney, "never recovered what the world calls cheerfulness."[84] So much for genetic possibilities. That Wallace was predisposed all his life to an eventual psychotic break is suggested by much of the foregoing. Hypersensitive, "reclusive" from childhood on, he was gifted with high literary productivity, yet bore within himself its very antithesis—a need for anonymity whose destructiveness his contemporaries were the first to recognize by calling it excessive "modesty" or "reticence." It is all projected in a fanciful story he wrote when he was barely nineteen, in which a dreamer sees the Temple of Memory and opening from it, behind a veil, the infinitely vaster Temple of Oblivion. Greatness is here also, as are all other human qualities. The dreamer sees a book, and in the story's concluding words, "I raised the volume, and, by the inscription on the back, perceived, to my ineffable dismay, that it was—*mine own writings!* Overwhelmed with horrour, I started and awoke."[85]

The news of his brother's death reached John Wallace two days before he was to sail. Horace Binney seemed unable to touch the specific details of his nephew's suicide even in the privacy of his diary, as he recorded on January 7:

On this day I received information of the death of my nephew Horace Binney Wallace in Paris, and much more to my grief & horror than to my surprise, that he fell by his own hand! His noble intellect had given way by overaction, by the breaking of his domestic society—break after break—by his rather morbid & overindulged aversion to the affectations, follies, insincerities, & ignorances of general society, and in the highest excitement of the Brain, he had rushed upon a sea voyage, & the *horrible solitude* of Paris, without a friend or support of any kind! God be merciful to us all![86]

In a subsequent passage he later deleted from his published obituary, Binney goes on to describe two human types—perhaps thinking of both of his Wallace nephews, John and Horace—those "given a calm & quiet spirit" and those "given a higher organization, a more exalted brain," who are capable in one moment of "the most beautiful & divine thoughts," and in the next, of "deluging the heart with unreal griefs, or frenzying the Brain into madness."

For such a passage would have strained the myth that Wallace had died of natural causes. These Binney described as "diseased cerebral action, induced by some lesion in the blood-vessels in the brain." John Wallace would repeat the formula in his "Memoir."

Other obituaries—several drawing on Binney's for substance—-joined in praise of Wallace's character and remarkable mental powers, lamenting that an early death had kept him from his promise, as one put it, "to be one of the brightest lights of our nation" (*ASPE*, xxix).

On January 7, Julia Ward Howe was still ignorant of her friend's death. She had met his cousin Horace Sargent the night before and wrote to Wallace: "I have been made happy by hearing that you are miserable in Paris . . . so anxious am I to have my best friend on the same side of the water with me again. . . . It was so un-

kind of you to go, and I miss you so much." She speaks of reading
Comte and Dante and having written two poems, which "lose half
their worth to me, for want of your criticism. I depend much upon
it—Your severity of taste has already helped me to write far better
than I could have written without it. You are, on this point, an
irreparable loss to me. . . . Enough of this, which is purely selfish
and egotistical. Far greater is my need of you as a friend. . . . You
promised to write from England—it is needless to remind you, false
Rosso, that you did not. *That* requires no excuse—your poor eyes
were too bad, or your spirits too low, or sea-sickness too recent. You
shall or shall not write to me from Paris, just as shall please you
best, but you must not forget me. I am too lonely, too helpless, too
orphaned to be deserted by you, my brother." She speaks of having
trouble with her own eyes, then concludes: "I am very thin and
ugly this winter—this alone consoles me for being unseen of you.
Farewell, my dear, dear friend—God bless you. Let me know, if
you can, when I may hope to see you again. Glaukó."[87]

She did not know his address. "You did not even leave me your
address, sinner," she scribbled on the letter, and proceeded to ask
her sister Annie, who had closer contact with Wallace's
Philadelphia friends and had perhaps just then arrived to see her.
Annie did not answer. Julia asked again, and then noticed that Annie had turned her face away to hide her tears.[88]

Perhaps no one mourned Wallace as much as did Julia Howe. In
her letter to Comte, who was personally unknown to her, she gave
vent to her feelings in French, confessing that she could not remain
on a plane of reason but must throw herself at Comte's feet and
cry: "Weep with me—console me!" Comte was clearly a surviving
symbol of her relationship to Wallace, the atheism she attributed to
him making her appeal only more frightening. "Ah, Monsieur, admit the soul's personal immortality—don't ravish my dead
friend—tell me that he lives again in the bosom of God."
Elsewhere in the letter, her account of what Wallace meant to her
dissolves now into a curious recitation of her accomplishments, now
into complaint about the barrenness of her life in America, now
into an appeal to Comte for his intellectual guidance.[89]

A few days later she wrote to her sister Louisa Crawford that
Wallace's death was the greatest loss she had experienced since the
death of their brother Henry. "Surely, surely, he was insane. I
believe it, and can almost fancy that I saw the elements of it in
some of his ways—but that, one is apt to do." To Louisa, she was

showing a quieter grief, saying: "My sensibilities are much exhausted. I shed few tears for him—it was rather like having had a limb amputated while under the influence of Chloroform, and then waking and feeling the loss in the *want*."[90]

She wrote of him in "Via Felice":

> I see him from the window
>   That ne'er my heart forgets;
> He buys from yonder maiden
>   My morning violets. . . .[91]

In March, John Wallace had his brother's remains transferred from Montmartre Cemetery to the family vault at St. Peter's Church in Philadelphia.

CHAPTER 2

"William Landor,"
Magazinist

I First Pieces

WALLACE seems to have made his magazine debut in the
New York Mirror during the latter part of 1835. Among
various unsigned essays and sketches, one on Scott in the
November 21 issue is almost certainly by him, for it is followed in
subsequent months by essays on Coleridge, Irving, Channing, and
Moore in the same manner, each signed by "William S. Somner."[1]
Elegance of expression is perhaps their chief characteristic. Rich,
figurative language abounds, and parallel sentences tend to take
the place of logical development. But they show critical insight as
well. The adulation bestowed on Scott is relieved by more reasoned
praise accorded to Coleridge, and in the remaining essays the
critical tone seems to grow progressively sharper. Thus a nice distinction appears in the essay on Irving, which might be taken as a
preliminary sketch for the more extended and self-assured article
Wallace would write on Irving fourteen years later: "He never
reasons; he wisely abstains from poetry: for he possesses a faculty
superior to reason and rarer than poetry, an intellectual genial
humour."

The essay on William Ellery Channing tends to fall into con-
tradictions, which is not surprising in view of Wallace's disparagement of Channing in his letter to his brother in 1840, followed by
his high praise in the pages of the *Home Journal* eight years later.
More unified and marked especially by inventive diction is the essay on Thomas Moore, who "paints always in enamel" and "sings
only for himself and to the fairies about him." Another essay,
"Scraps from the Notebook of a Pedant,"[2] deserves a word here for
its meticulous linguistic observations, which, incidentally, show a

sensitivity not only to the tradition but also to the development of English. Here Wallace seems to make his first, richly illustrated comment on plagiarism: "The most popular poets have been the greatest thieves, as Gray and Byron."

Wallace's scholarship is given full expression in "The Authorship of the Doctor," which appeared in the *Knickerbocker Magazine* in November, 1836.[3] When the first volumes of *The Doctor,* Southey's immense rambling novel, had begun to appear in the 1830's, an avid reading public speculated about Isaac D'Israeli, Sir Egerton Brydges, Hartley Coleridge, and Southey himself among others as the possible author.[4] Poe for one declared on reviewing the first volumes in July, 1836, "We cannot think Southey wrote it, but have no idea who did."[5]

The nineteen-year-old Wallace's article was no doubt as perplexing in its own anonymity as it was convincing in its scholarly demonstration. Arguing against the authorship of Hartley Coleridge on the grounds of his Whig politics and his insufficient learning, Wallace gives evidence in the work of Southey's habits of thinking, his prejudices, and his verbal peculiarities. But most impressive is the lengthy presentation of passages from *The Doctor* set against passages from Southey's other writings. On both sides, Wallace points out, a Tory argues for legal reform and, although a religious man, opposes Sunday schools and Bible societies. Both sides condemn manufactories, alehouses, newspapers, free trade, poor-laws, work in brick kilns, and the use of children as chimney sweeps. Both ridicule phrenology; both show a great command of Italian, Spanish, and English literature. It is said that Southey himself, while still denying having written *The Doctor* and ascribing it to a clever imitator, expressed interest in the authorship of the demonstration (*LC*, 103 - 4). But if so, there is no indication that it was ever revealed to him.

"Lord Bolingbroke," touched on, in the previous chapter, was also written in 1836. This meditation on the darker aspects of genius with its somewhat self-conscious Johnsonian rhetoric was in the pages of *Stanley* to establish "William Landor" in Poe's eyes as a Bolingbroke authority. Whether "Rosicrucian Philosophy" (*LC*, 173 - 87), which belongs to the same year, ever appeared in a periodical is not known. Believing the Abbé de Montfaucon de Villiars's anonymous *Le Comte de Gabalis* (1670) to be the chief source of English writers on gnomes, sylphs, nymphs, and salamanders, Wallace tries in his essay to remedy the obscurity into which this work has fallen since Pope's praise for it in the Preface to his "Rape of the Lock."

The following year Wallace completed a series of dialogues, which, according to an editorial note in *Literary Criticisms* (p. 245), were meant as a contribution to a work by a college friend. More likely, John Wallace, the author of the note, was honoring his brother's wish to disassociate himself from *Stanley*.[6] Since the dialogues were eventually incorporated into that novel and *Henry Pulteney*, they will be examined in connection with those works.

"Sermon in the Garden," written in the same year, appeared anonymously in *Godey's Lady's Book* in February, 1838.[7] Somewhat self-indulgent in its length and density, it is a fruition of that sensitivity to nature which we have noted in Wallace from early childhood. Rising to a tribute to Wordsworth, the "Sermon" celebrates nature as the source of beauty, wisdom, and virtue. The garden is as fit a place to worship as any church, for God "may be seen in the earth, and seen in the sky, and all creation's forms are frost-worked with his love" (*LC*, 385). Emerson's *Nature*, which appeared two years previously, may have had an influence on this essay; but where Emerson expands the meaning of "nature" to include human action, Wallace makes as careful a distinction between the two as he makes between God and His works, in his sharply critical comments about Channing. Thus the garden is never identified with Transcendental nature but remains the church it sought to replace.

"Life," or "Our Little Life," as the essay appeared after Wallace's death in the *Ladies' Repository*,[8] is pivoted on Sir Thomas Browne's "Man is a noble animal! splendid in ashes. . . ." The Brownesque strain continues as Wallace muses on man's dual glory and insignificance. The world is at one point strikingly envisioned as "a material sneer. . . . I imagine that a smile awoke the angels from nothingness, and that man was laughed into being" (*LC*, 382). But the Christian call to duty at the end is tacked on rather gratuitously.

"Religion and Poetry" appeared in *Burton's Gentleman's Magazine* in April, 1838.[9] It was signed "Landor," since with the previous month's installment of *Henry Pulteney* in the same publication, "William Landor" had begun its brief existence. What made Wallace choose this name we do not know. Whether he had Walter Savage Landor in mind, with whom future readers would confuse him—as in a footnote appended by Poe to "The Mystery of Marie Rogêt"—is an open question.

Based on the premise that intellect and feeling must be kept distinct, "Religion and Poetry" begins with a fanciful anecdote set in Persia, then proceeds to show that religious poetry is "full of evil." The argument is historical and shows a partiality for Protestantism as against Catholicism. For as the Greeks made the feelings into a religion that finally fell slave to passion, so the Catholic Church through the Virgin and the saints extended religion into a system of feelings until it became corrupt. The Protestant's "repent and believe" is sufficient for religion. Poetry must be kept apart from Christianity, as it is in such poets as Wordsworth, Coleridge, and Shelley. This way, "the golden lies of the poet"—"though not accepted by the intellect"—can be "of infinite benefit in keeping open in our breasts the springs of wonder, and preserving in the world some traces of mystery." (*LC*, 398). Wallace with his analytic mind liked to keep entities apart. The essay brings to mind T. S. Eliot's "Religion and Literature." In Eliot's view all great literature serves "the primacy of the supernatural over the natural life" and is therefore fundamentally "religious," or in some cases "*un*consciously Christian," but his disagreement with Wallace is only a theological one—almost one of definitions. As critics they both prefer poets who are not religious in the narrower sense of Vaughan, or Crashaw, or Herbert.

II "*The Most Remarkable Novel of the Century*"

Published some forty years after Charles Brockden Brown's series of Gothic novels, *Stanley* is an example—as are many of Poe's and some of Hawthorne's works—of this persistent mode in American fiction. More importantly, *Stanley* is a novel of education or initiation. What the Gothic trappings mask is nothing less than organized crime, and the dramatic function of its leader, Tyler, is precisely to effect the young hero's growth from sheltered innocence to worldly experience. Finally, *Stanley* is a novel of ideas, or more precisely, a novel in which action alternates with ideas expressed through a series of superimposed dialogues.

Wallace probably wrote these first, then the dramatic part of the novel between 1837 and 1838. According to one reviewer, he submitted the manuscript to Lea and Blanchard—who had expressed interest in the idea some years previously—in several portions, sending each mysteriously through a different channel. How his publishers communicated with him in turn—in order to pay him, for example—remains a mystery also.[10]

Stanley; or the Recollections of a Man of the World appeared in the fall of 1838,[11] in two volumes bound in maroon linen, and caused a literary sensation. *Snowden's Ladies' Companion,* the magazine that was four years later to serialize Poe's "Mystery of Marie Rogêt," considered the book superior to many of those "flowing so fast from the press of our country."[12] The *Expositor,* a recently established magazine in New York, spoke of it as "decidedly the best book of the season."[13] Horace Greeley's weekly *New Yorker* began its three-column review: "This is in many respects the most remarkable novel which has appeared in this century."[14] The *New York Review* regarded it "a work of genius."[15] *Burton's Gentleman's Magazine,* four months after blasting Poe's *Narrative of Arthur Gordon Pym,* called *Stanley* "decidedly the most forcible and original work of the day."[16]

In view of the almost total absence of *Stanley* from any subsequent critical or historical account of the American novel, such praise may be surprising. But the reviews expressed reservations also. The *New Yorker,* after dwelling on the cleverness, instructiveness, and profundity of *Stanley,* raised the question of its general readability. *Burton's* complained that "the rust of the scholar is too plainly discernible, and the metaphysical subtleties and abstruse niceties of the German schools preponderate over the wisdom of the man of the world." The *New York Review* made a more precise diagnosis: "There is a want of proportion between the mysterious elements of the story and these long conversations: they come in at the very time when the excited imagination of the reader cannot wait to hear them." Still, these reviewers only saw more or less darkly what in subsequent decades would crystallize into a critical principle. In an age when fiction and the essay lived more happily together, a book such as *Stanley* could be published and praised. For the modern reader it is really two books welded together to their mutual disadvantage.

The narrative element comprises roughly three-fourths. From the vantage point of the "calm and lake-like tranquillity of senescence," Stanley looks back to narrate the events of his early life. He is the son of a man of rank, wealth, and talent, who after a sudden reverse in fortune has been compelled to retreat from the city to the humble village of Merton. Here Stanley spends his childhood and early youth in study and meditation, rarely seeking society, emerging from among his books only to meet and fall in love with Emily Wilson. But Stanley feels he is unworthy of her; he must prove himself before asking for her hand, and he decides to devote three more years to the cultivation of his mind. He enters college and begins to write—first poetry, a volume of which appears anonymously and wins wide acclaim, then fiction and every other branch of prose. At the conclusion of these three years Stanley has achieved literary eminence, and proud and ardent, he returns to Merton to fly into Emily's arms. But the young girl receives him with a certain reserve, which Stanley takes to be a change of heart. He does not yield to his first shock of melancholy. He returns to the city, there "to profess for a while the business of pleasure, and to take the flowing waters of life."

But contact with the world also offers young Stanley the uncomfortable realization that he has enemies. A document he has received from his father, which is the death-bed confession of a certain Thompson, a man directly responsible for the Stanley family's financial ruin, brings Stanley into conflict with Thompson's former associates, a powerful criminal organization. Tyler, their brilliant and unscrupulous leader, has won Stanley's confidence and, in order to have the young man more completely in his power, has turned the now loving Emily against him so that one evening she refuses to admit him. Although Tyler openly professes that Christianity and truth are irreconcilable, Stanley, who believes that "genius is ever essentially magnanamous," cannot think of him in terms of practical evil until one night he witnesses Tyler's presence at one of the gang's secret meetings.

Tyler, who has stolen the Thompson document from under Stanley's pillow, has a quarrel of his own with the gang and disappears. Leaderless, the gang disintegrates. Stanley's party sets out to the dying Thompson but arrives just as he has been strangled. Stanley's hope of recovering the family fortune is for the present lost, and he finds solace in retiring with Emily, his bride, from "the tedious bustle" in which he has been living.

Sometime later Tyler's message arrives: "The period of my death is near, and I have documents to deliver to you as well as explanations to make which concern you deeply." Stanley is guided through wild forests and precipitous hills to Tyler's mansion, where the dying man restores the Stanley fortune and gives a long account of his life, from which he has in his mad thirst for power eliminated human feeling. Having been brought by nameless terrors to the final understanding that conscience is an indubitable fact of existence, Tyler dies.

Such a plot is characteristic of the period, as is the arrangement of dramatic detail. Suspense is chiefly physical, making use of disguise, concealment, and the rate at which horses will bear their riders, while a Gothic atmosphere pervades all. The numerous secret passageways, underground dungeons, and massive pillars are matched in eeriness only by the moonlit outdoors:

The shade was deep and concealed me perfectly, while the objects beyond were exhibited with meridian clearness. . . . After a short pause a man came out and closed the door carefully behind him. He was enveloped in a long cloak, with a broad hat over his eyes and very large whiskers and moustaches. . . . He turned down the avenue, and to my dismay came directly towards me. I remained breathless in my concealment. (I, 84)

Of Stanley's psychological growth there are distinct stages. The picture he exhibits at his father's house is that of a young man untouched by experience, reading without direction, afraid to think. "I found literature the best refuge from the fatigue of thought and the yet greater fatigue of idleness" (I, 16). It is not surprising that on his single excursion into society he should fall in love, that viewing life through the prism of love he should be exalted. The "airy company" of books seems now to him only half vital. Yet he has also come to understand the importance of education, and at college he lets thoughts of reuniting with Emily inspire, but not interfere with, his intellectual labors. He lives alone and does not mingle with others. For study has become for him a serious business, a preparation for authorship.

I read none but the best, and I read them with the utmost attention. I studied them closely, penetrated their merits, and saw wherein their greatness consisted. I had formerly approached them with the coldness of an admirer; I now followed their steps with something of the daring of a rival. I wrote on for a long time, developing my thoughts on various subjects, and acquiring power and ease in the use of language. . . . I lived in a dreamy whirl of excitement. My intellect seemed to expand, and I grasped confidently things which formerly I would not have ventured to approach. (I, 24 - 25)

But that these years have been, nevertheless, lived in an essentially naive state becomes evident to Stanley when he returns to Emily. He enters her parlor.

She sat alone, fully dressed, upon a sofa, reading a newspaper. She raised her eye, and as she recognized me, smiled, and with a very composed air advanced toward me.
"Mr. Stanley!" giving me her hand, "I am extremely happy to see you. Pray sit down. When did you arrive in town?"
"Lately,—immediately," said I.
"You found the roads very dusty, I am afraid. We are very much in want of rain."
"Very,—extremely so, indeed:" I replied, absolutely stunned by the calm immobility of the speaker. . . . Great God! the being whom I had enshrined in the seventh heaven of idolatry. . . . I knew not whether to laugh or cry. (I, 33 - 34)

Stanley returns to the city amidst "sensations of deep shame and mortification," but he masters these emotions. "From the jarring chaos came manliness and strength" (I, 35). He is now in many ways "a man of the world," as the subtitle promises. He meets Emily at a fashionble watering place and is able to study her calmly, realizing that the vehement emotions of love are never kindled by a real person but by a "representative phantasm." And the manner of the narration becomes light and flamboyant:

There is no business, by the way, that I am acquainted with, more entertaining than that of furnishing a house, especially if you are a poor man; for it calls forth the greatest pleasure of which man is capable—the pleasure of running in debt. . . .
The sense of boundless domination with which one enters a shop—be it book-store, or other, where one's credit is yet good . . . the heroic and soul-ennobling resolutions and cheering schemes for getting the money by the time it is due . . . all form a rare and admirable combination of pleasures. . . . We may amuse misfortune, as Bolingbroke did his exile, by recounting those that have been in like predicament: we may remember how Mirabeau was "*obéré de dettes,*"—how Talleyrand could not pay for his white carriage, the tastefullest in all Paris . . . how Byron had an execution in his house eight times during the first year of his marriage, and how his beds were taken, and how he stamped on his grandmother's watch, and ground it to atoms in a fit of despair. . . . (I, 92 - 94)

Only in matters of evil is Stanley still unsophisticated. Between a gang of scoundrels that try to fleece him at the gaming table and Tyler, whose eloquent denunciation of Christian values frightens and fascinates him, he cannot bring himself to see a connection. For Tyler is a gentleman. Then Stanley makes his shocking discovery:

That extraordinary person, at the depth of whose learned thoughts and the keenness of whose fine philosophical perceptions I had been so often impressed and delighted—the patient thinker, the laborious scholar, the brilliant wit—had been and was a bold, daring, systematic and successful actor in the darkest scenes of daring and was habitually occupied with the rude and stern strivings of worldliness and crime. (II, 63)

Of the world Stanley has nothing more to learn. Later when the dying Tyler tells his own life story Stanley listens without offering a single question. Tyler's account is for him a mere recapitulation of what he has already come to know.

Notwithstanding the high praise that the *New Yorker* accorded to *Stanley*, it objected to Tyler's characterization, calling it "unreal." Today, with a clearer perspective toward romantic fiction, the reader is more prone to accept Tyler as a legitimate part of the total machinery. True, he is in some ways an abstraction, but as such he forms an interesting antithesis to Stanley; furthermore it is through Tyler that *Stanley* can claim structurally to be a novel of ideas.

When Tyler begins to tell his story in the last chapter he gives an importance to childhood in the formation of character that strikes the reader as modern. He was born on the western coast of England—"in that wild and impressive region of solitude and beauty." His parents were rich and well-born, but he was cursed by a "morbid sensibility," which made him subject to "dark passions and blind sufferings," so that his childhood seems to him "a dark and confused memory of pain." His parents were no solace:

My father was a man of that thoroughness of art and breeding that you might have doubted whether he had ever been a boy. My mother was a person of rare and powerful intellect. . . . But she had no feeling, and she laughed at those who had it; indeed, her contempt for all softness of heart often coarsened a conversation otherwise refined and rich to the last degree of delightfulness. . . . From her I met with only taunts which my tenderness quick turned to torture, and cold repulses which outraged all my power of endurance. (II, 207 - 8)

The happier, more serene Stanley was able to absorb the pangs of love so that they became part of his education. When young Tyler's father made him lose the girl he loved, "I gnashed my teeth with rage," crying, " 'I will combat my calamity, and strangle the life of suffering within me' " (II, 218). For suffering, Tyler explains, comes from feeling, and feeling is not the mere impression an object or incident makes on us but the heart's resistance to it. Suffering can thereby be overcome by allowing external stimuli to have a "free swing through the breast" without opposition. Applying this psychological discovery, which, incidentally, comes close to what is understood today by the interaction of ego and superego, Tyler was able to attain "that majesty of moral freedom which is mental power. . . . God had no more control of me. . . . Henceforth, there were two of us to reign" (II, 221).

Free of love and fear, his heart "darkened into a demon of ambition." Placing himself even above fate, which is a mere collection of puny, inferior wills, he set about to conquer the world. A careful calculator of human motives, he knew "that the subjugation of mankind to the wishes and purposes of an individual, which is what ambition craves, is less the forging of a chain than the brandishing of a whip; for men are born in slavery and cradled in thraldom" (II, 229). Yet in place of open conquest, Tyler preferred anonymity. "I mingled deeply and extensively in the intrigue of European courts, and participated in the more ardent passions of Asiatic empires" (II, 245). When he became bored by those pursuits he came to America, organized his gang, and went after the Stanley fortune.

Now by returning the Stanley documents he is in his old age repudiating his life of crime. He has been troubled lately by nameless terrors. Not unlike Mozart's Don Giovanni, another great defier of both feeling and morality,

"Though I deny a deity and laugh at hell, there is not a moment that I do not think of God and judgment. . . .

"My life is unbalanced and overthrown; I dwell in a state of moral madness. . . .

"Of late . . . I have had mysterious visitations of a dark horror which I cannot comprehend. . . . I would combat with it, but I cannot. . . . Yet I will maintain my being. . . . It may torture, but I will bear; and as I do not struggle, I cannot be defeated. It cannot annihilate.—He comes. Stand still;—he comes only for me."

. . . With his clenched hand extended, and his teeth firmly set, he advanced two steps forward, as if he drove an enemy before him; then tottered for a moment, and fell lifeless on the floor. (II, 251 - 56)

Of the rest of the characters there is little to say. "The whole of
the characters speak in the same language," complained the
reviewer for *Burton's*, "and indulge in flights of fancy far beyond
the probability of their stations. The poorest and lowest talk logic,
quote Latin and Milton, and revel in the wisdom of the fathers."
Again, from a more modern perspective it might be argued that a
novel of ideas allows for a certain degree of stylization in this
regard; but there is a lack of development, or realism, or three-
dimensionality in some of the characters such as Emily. She is too
ready to believe evil of Stanley without having even the curiosity to
listen to her lover defend himself. Yet the novel has much general-
ized psychological insight, such as the analysis of two types of love:
"a passion which begins in disinterestedness and ends in self-
sacrifice" and "an affection which in the morning gladness of its
fresh vigor is so exquisitely delicious that it might be deemed an
ecstasy of selfishness."

Poe's observation that Wallace is a "stiff" and "pedantic"
writer[17] might be modified by the passages in which the narrative
style ranges from the introspective to the dramatic to the flamboyant. Sometimes the comic touches the absurd, as in the following reply by a Mr. Jones, whom Stanley questions on galvanic
currents at a ball: "The best exposition of that hypothesis . . . is to
be found in a volume on Galvanism, published by Longman,
Hurst, Rees, Orme, Brown, Green and Longman, Paternoster Row,
London, 1826, twelve-mo, hot-pressed, one volume, price ten
shillings, boards (I, 155).

All in all, atmosphere, suspense, and most importantly, the
dramatic and ideological confrontation between Stanley and Tyler
generate enough power to absorb the weaknesses noted so far.
Stanley is more seriously marred by an undigested intellectual content which Wallace chose to keep within the novel proper rather
than relegating it to the already extraneous dialogues. As long as
Tyler speaks in character the reader listens. For example, "Religion
is a disease of the mind. . . . Will you call that natural to man
with which he never sympathises save in the hour of his sickness
and suffering?" (I, 197). But Wallace will make Tyler the
mouthpiece for just about any idea. It is thus that the Bolingbroke
essay appears here—introduced with a "by-the-by" and supplied
with four sets of quotation marks for alternate recitation by Stanley
and Tyler (I, 216 - 21). Still more incongruous is Tyler's inordinate-
ly long praise of the American system of government with its feeble

justification: "I am interested as a philosopher in the game that is playing" (I, 69). In itself a perceptive piece of writing, which contrasts the constitutionally devised minimality of the American government with the inherently greater scope of the government in England, it is obviously grafted onto the novel—rather carelessly too, the Englishman Tyler being allowed at one point to call America "our republic."

III   The Dialogues

But the total intellectual content of *Stanley,* which caused reviewers to acclaim it despite their own objections to some of its formal aspects, is scarcely indicated by the foregoing. Four times in the course of the narration the action is suspended so that the reader may get altogether one hundred and ten pages (out of a total five hundred) of those literary and philosophical discussions previously mentioned, involving scenes and speakers that remain for the most part outside the novel. Yet they are the source of some of Wallace's most interesting ideas and cannot be neglected here. Although the dialogues touch on many subjects, such as the philosophy of dining or the Greek Anthology or the excessive democratization of American society, a single theme is dominant: the narrator's changing attitude from rejection to acceptance of the Romantic poets. Since Wallace expressed unqualified admiration for Coleridge in the *New York Mirror* as early as 1835, this change in the narrator seems more dramatized than autobiographical—unless the first dialogue was written appreciably earlier than the rest. In any case, the dialogues are an interesting reflection of the times, for by the latter part of the 1830's American criticism has passed through successive stages of enthusiasm for Pope, Byron, and Wordsworth.[18] In this sense too, then, *Stanley* is a novel of initiation.

The first dialogue[19] takes place on the seashore, between the narrator and William Herand (in the first version, Robert Courteney), a young poet, who is nevertheless without "that moodiness of feeling and that lawlessness of passion" which Byron and Moore have taught the world as indispensible for poetic character. Thus the main theme of the dialogue is suggested: the superiority of Pope to the Romantic poets. After the speakers pay tribute to the sea as a "type and token of Almighty power" and speculate on immortality, they return to Pope's great dictum that "the proper study of mankind is man." Herand, an avowed classicist, admires Pope's poetry of "valuable moral reflection"—his "white light of unrefracted truth"—as he admires Pope the man "withdrawing himself from the world, and nursing in solitude the fire of his heart . . . with no vices, with few foibles; free from domestic cares, and safe from all political disturbances; wasting not a moment on the transitory."[20]

By contrast, "look at Shelley complaining of wrong and tyranny and eulogizing purity and heavenly love, and then marrying two wives and leaving one of them to die of a broken heart.[21] Look at Coleridge,—who together with Wordsworth is essentially of the same tribe,—writing songs 'that bid the heavens be mute,' and leaving his wife to the charity of Mr. Southey" (I, 52; *LC*, 252). The Romantic poets speak much about invention and imagination, "but it is yet to be proved that a subject rises in poetic value in proportion as it sinks in every other value" (I, 51; *LC*, 251).

But Byron is Herand's chief target. In contrast to Pope's "white light," Byron's flashes proceed from broken rays. Byron's penetration into the human heart only appears deeper than Pope's because of its narrowness. With his deep fascination for Byron, which will subsequently emerge, Wallace here makes Herand complain of Byron's "dyspeptic Laras and costive Giaours. . . . No admiration to which the genius of Byron might prompt me, could ever check the repulsive scorn which is stirred within me by the sight of one thus having 'his eyes forever on himself,' and coming before the world only to tell it how keen are his sensibilities and how painful his indigestions; that he has not loved the world, and that Wordsworth is his aversion" (I, 56; *LC*, 256 - 57). Clearly, Byron's ego is grating against Wallace's as Herand cries: "Never will I so far debase my own inward dignity as to listen and applaud the miserable petulant outbreakings of a disappointed and jealous lordling."[22]

The second dialogue, taking place at a Mr. Benton's dinner party, is both longer and looser than the first. There is at first some vivid pictorial rendering of the guests, but there is little effort to keep them visibly or in any other way delineated as their voices resound. The discussion begins with the aesthetics of dining. The host establishes the vital distinction between appetite and taste, one of the guests compares a well-cooked meal to a symphony by Beethoven, and another speculates on constructing "a gamut of odors." For the soul, according to Plato, is harmony; as a mental perception of relations gives rise to the sciences, so a physical, or sensuous, perception of relations gives rise to the fine arts. Metaphysically they are but one. Since mathematics is "the science of pure and abstract relation," it is conceivable that a formula might be constructed to express a temple or an overture—in fact, "all that man can think on all subjects" (I, 108 - 9; *LC,* 269 - 70). It may not be an exaggeration to say that Einstein's Unified Field Theory in the next century would spring from a similar vision. But if Wallace expressed such faith in mathematics in 1837, he made a sharp reversal by 1838, for at one point in the novel Tyler says that mathematics, being concerned only with relations, "has no regard to the nature and qualities of the things related," and that therefore "the axioms of mathematics are not axioms of general truth" (I, 206). Since Poe was so taken by this passage that he copied it into his "Purloined Letter," more must be said about it in the next chapter.

The art of dining pursues its course to the ancients. The Greeks, who believed that perfection lay in all-inclusiveness and painted their buildings and statues, committed a similar excess in bringing musicians into the dining room. The Romans, on the other hand, "did these things very handsomely," and reference is made via Suetonius to a dinner given by Vitellius, where a dish in the center contained "the livers of scari, the brains of pheasants and peacocks, the tongues of parrots, and the bellies of lamprey eels" (I, 112; *LC,* 273). One of the guests associates genius with a love of good eating, another virtue, but a third counters with an anecdote about the great epicure, Dartineuf, who committed the base villainy of stealing out to a friend's garden and plucking and eating *both* of his perfectly ripe plums. After the guests establish that the perfect age for a cook is forty, the conversation turns to literature.

The critical judgments that are voiced may or may not agree with modern opinion, but the talk maintains both the brisk tempo and the urbanity of the previous passages. The opinions, cerebral or personal, range with ease among the authors, showing Wallace's vast reading and considerable conversational skill. From among the eighteenth-century critics, Dr. Johnson is singled out for particular praise; his *Lives of the Poets* is compared to "a rock in the ocean" amidst "the waves and waters of opinion" (I, 119; *LC,* 284). But Boswell is somewhat underestimated. The man with the most John-sonian integrity now alive is found to be Daniel Webster, and the company drink to his health. Webster, incidentally, was a personal

friend of the Wallaces and was later to bestow high praise on
Horace Wallace in turn.[23] Byron emerges, a target once again for
some of the older, more conservative voices, but now the narrator
defends Byron's genius, speaking of certain scenes in *Manfred* as
being worthy of Shakespeare. Interestingly, these scenes are Manfred's attempted suicide and subsequent meeting with the witch, to
whom he says that "an all-pitiless demon held him back,—back by
a single hair which would not break"(I, 125; *LC*, 290).

The victim of general, undeviating critical abuse is Bulwer. He
warrants consideration, not because of the company's colorful invectives: Bulwer is Byron's literary offspring, "as the Mahometans
believe the pig to have been generated from the excrement of the
elephant"; or, "Bulwer mimics Byron's depravity . . . forgetting
that an ass wears a cloven foot as well as the devil" (I, 126; *LC*,
291). But through the specific charges against Bulwer, there
emerges Wallace's theory of the novel.[24] Bulwer is said to be too
emotionally charged and to write "always in *issimo*" (I, 127, *LC*,
292). Unlike a great novelist like Scott, who is always above his
subject, Bulwer allows himself to be overmastered by the emotion
of the subject. His style is so ornate as to be vicious, and he
dramatizes generalizations. "In an epigram we may say, meta-
phorically and extremely, that a man never means a compliment
but he makes an insult; but to introduce a Lord Aspeden actually
making every speech throughout a long conversation, an elaborate
rudeness, is totally to mistake the limits of art" (I, 128 - 29; *LC*,
293 - 94). His characters are unbelievable because they violate the
rule that "fact is the field of the historian and probability of the
romance-writer"—or poet, one might add, as Aristotle put it. The
fault is given a perceptive modern diagnosis: "It is a want of psychological truth." In fact, poets—Byron specifically—can afford a
certain "strangeness" of characters, since they move in "wild and
imaginary scenes," but the novelist's characters, "being on the terra
firma of a brick pavement, and breathing the common air of cities,
are within a far narrower law." Finally, Bulwer renders his
characters subjectively, not as they are; and "he describes, rather
than exhibits them. . . . The secret of his failure is that he is too
much of a metaphysician to be a dramatist" (I, 129 - 32; *LC*, 294 -
97).

Does this last statement contain a concerned allusion to *Stanley*
itself? Bulwer's "failure," at any rate, can only have been an artistic one, for he was extremely popular. The concept is more

applicable to the more thoroughgoing failure of Sir Egerton Brydges, who "did not master his genius" but let his creative impulse lead him to others' works rather than his own. As for genius, although the following passage is offered as an answer to an attack on Coleridge,[25] it might be a model—and perhaps was—for Horace Binney's anguished analysis of his nephew's death:

The strong seductions and fierce trials of the heart of genius who shall estimate? Such men are in a raging tumult even from their very birth; they are living always in the midst of tempests, and never, during life, enjoy the blessing of clear vision or calm touch. . . . What does an ordinary mind know of the inner storm . . . of restlessness,—the craving after excitement and high action,—the . . . widowed longing after sympathy? . . . Existence is to such men anguish; every pulse is pain; their breath is a sigh. (I, 139 - 40; *LC*, 304)

The third dialogue takes place in Mr. Woodward's library. When the narrator enters, his elderly host is "reclining on the sofa and musing with half closed eyes over a volume of the Greek Anthology," which with its simplicity and sincerity is the "confessional" of the Greeks, in contrast to the heroic utterances of their histories, epics, and tragedies. The conversation turns to the ancients' moral principles, which are sometimes rejected when Christianity is rejected. Breaking with his earlier preference for Protestantism, which he expressed in "Religion and Poetry," Wallace seems here to embark on a life-long interest in Catholicism, which Mr. Woodward prefers, along with heathenism, to Protestantism, because they take a more favorable view of "religious feeling." "In the mistaken view of the Protestant Christians, God is a being to be dreaded, and to be worshipped from a distance" (II, 29; *LC*, 317). Henry Adams was similarly to connect Venus and the Virgin as desirable intercessors.[26]

Mr. Woodward is a conservative, as one might expect, displeased with the current trend of widespread democratization. He bewails "this insane craving after 'knowledge,' this diseased exaggeration of the value of facts." It is but the mistaking of information for education, which is now deprived of "the only essential things, the principles of religion and the rules of duty." He bewails further "this disgusting flattery and stimulation of the mob; this admission of the worthless and scorn-compelling rabble to the decision of questions which they can never comprehend; this breaking of principles over the back of majorities" (II, 32; *LC*, 320). Wallace is perhaps nowhere else more scornful of Jacksonian democracy than in this passage. In fact, the narrator interjects, "it is the matter of statistical evidence, that an increase of crime has attended the increase of knowledge." Mr. Woodward offers as an explanation "the dissemination of cheap magazines and cyclopedias" which has deprived the simple man of the beneficial effects of "natural meditation," leaving him "too busy to think, too excited to feel." (II, 35 - 36; *LC*, 323 - 24).

If the antagonism between intellect and virtue is hinted at here, it is but a step away from the plight of the poet. He is in a worse position than the "ordinary man" who makes his feelings "the beacon and guide of his conduct." The poet "observes his feelings only to portray them"; in short, he is an amoralist, if not immoralist (II, 37; *LC*, 325). Again, as in the previous dialogue, the tone becomes more and more personal. Authorship is called "the most hapless trade" yet invented. "To write for one's livelihood,—to stimulate the weary and over-tasked mind at the call of necessity" is agony. And little admiration reaches personally even the most fortunate writer. "In the case of a great poet, the sensibility which he pictures excites and wears his own"; even if he is physically comfortable, imaginatively he is suffering. The obvious illustration is Byron, whose "sacrifice to fame was the most awful that ever was made—his own heart" (II, 38 - 39; *LC*, 325 - 26). And yet ultimately—still in a personal context—the miseries of a life of reflection are preferable to the miseries of a life of action.

With the fourth dialogue Wallace made some effort to integrate the setting and the speakers into the main action of the novel. The narrator, his friend Seward (originally Herbert), and Henry Thompson are on their way to the dying Thompson, who is now made rather incongruously Henry's brother. They are on horseback and presumably in a hurry, but that does not affect their leisurely discussion about the Romantic poets, which in the previous version was given a more appropriate setting of the Lake District in England.

"The eye is the best of artists," wrote Emerson in *Nature;* and there is a similar subjectivism, almost Transcendentalism, in the initial idea here, inspired by the splendor of the morning, that the miracle of creation is not a single event in the past but forever repeated. Emersonian also is the assertion that as earthly beauty depends on the sky, so man's higher thoughts are "the airs and odors of an immortal world." The mind is all: "by degrees, all the external world shall be transformed into internal convictions . . . and all material existence be *thought* into God" (II, 72 - 73; *LC*, 332 - 33).

God leads to the soul and the soul to Coleridge, whose struggles with opium "gave him capacity to behold the tints of sin and purity in their broadest and deepest contrast" (II, 76; *LC*, 336). But Coleridge is briefly touched; Wallace is more interested in contrasting Byron and Shelley. In Byron, personal feelings were "elevated and refined into the ideal . . . Shelley's feelings were in his imagination, and he had no personality. . . . Byron succeeded by the magnitude of his failure. He wrote true poetry without being a poet. . . . The other was a born bard." Ultimately, notwithstanding Shelley's greater original poetic genius, Byron through his "victorious will" emerged the greater poet (II, 81 - 82; *LC*, 340 - 41).

Then Byron is examined with reference to his influence, and the picture darkens. Byron is seen as "the forerunner and herald of the advent of some new, deep, fervid epoch which shall develop in action that struggling energy which his verses show, and be as violent, as free, and as selfish as he was" (II, 84; *LC*, 343). And Wallace touches on the figure who is to preoccupy him more and more in his future writings: Napoleon. As Byron released the forces of "liberty and strength and madness" in literature, so Napoleon did in politics. "That agitation has subsided, but I think that another, slower, calmer, more general, and stronger swell is setting in" to complete its work (II, 84 - 85; *LC*, 343 - 44). The conservative consciousness is both fearful and fascinated.

Wordsworth seems easier to admire for the "dignity which he gives to common things" (II, 96; *LC*, 354). Wordsworth has in fact finally come into his own through these dialogues. It is pointed out that he is serene; in him there is "none of the narrow sympathy and bigoted enthusiasm of the school of passionists" (II, 88; *LC*, 346). More extensive quotations than employed in any of the previous dialogues illustrate Wordsworth's charity and his faith. Here perhaps one becomes more aware also of the limitations of much early nineteenth-century criticism with its emphasis on moral teaching. Poe had just recently made the revolutionary declaration that the aim of poetry is not truth but pleasure;[27] but Wallace is still under the spell of traditional critical thinking, especially when reading the Romantic poet with the quietest voice.

With a great deal of critical good will, then, it is possible to identify the narrator in each of these dialogues with Stanley and consider them the intellectual counterpart of the education he acquires in the field of experience. Since there is a strong moral tone running through all four dialogues, one can certainly relate them thematically to the action flowing around them. More specifically, certain literary and philosophical subjects do recur both inside and outside the dialogues, as do certain less tangible conversational moods; in the third dialogue, the comparison between a life of reflection and a life of action is especially applicable to the process of Stanley's dual education. Such was undoubtedly Wallace's own justification for their inclusion; although one must bear in mind also that the novels of Thomas Love Peacock with their extraneous dialogues, not to speak of Southey's rambling novel, *The Doctor*, probably served Wallace as precedents. It would appear from his keen criticism of Bulwer's novels that Wallace would eventually see his error in this area; but the question still remains whether he repudiated *Stanley* for such objective critical reasons.

His reasons may have been personal ones. Since there are obvious autobiographical elements in *Stanley*, such as the loss of family fortune compelling a retreat from the city to the village of Merton, it is likely that there are others less easy to identify. Whether or not Wallace had a recognizable model for Tyler, for example, it seems certain that the conception of Tyler is a personal one. As counterparts, Stanley and Tyler are rooted in certain similarities: both are sensitive intellectuals with a taste for solitude and introspection, both are well-born, both suffer disappointment in love. It is especially interesting to note that whereas Stanley's mother died early, Tyler's mother was a woman of powerful intellect but no feeling. Now Wallace was deprived of his mother's habitual presence from his ninth year on; she was a woman whom her brother, Horace Binney, who had initiated her departure from her sons, described as brilliant; and Horace Binney himself has been described as brilliant but cold. The hypothesis easily suggests itself that Wallace felt a Binney coldness near his own heart and dramatized it into the villain Tyler, perhaps unconsciously. The extreme secrecy in which he submitted his manuscript to the publishers suggests more deep-seated discomfort than ordinary shyness. And, significantly also, John Wallace, who after his brother's death spared no effort to secure his literary fame, observed his brother's life-long wish to let *Stanley* remain unacknowledged.[28]

IV Henry Pulteney

As a serialized novel depending on the separate impact of each installment, Henry Pulteney,[29] though linear in construction, is heavily plotted. About one-third the length of Stanley, its central conflict is once again between good and evil, first through the villain Harford's pursuit of Pulteney, then through Pulteney's pursuit of Harford. The enmity between these two arises when Henry Pulteney, an Englishman, falls in love with his cousin Lilly and a few days later brings a certain highwayman to justice. For, as a consequence of Pulteney's attentions, Lilly rejects the suit of Harford, who is none other than the unfortunate highwayman's son. Harford strikes back by spreading evil gossip about Pulteney so that Lilly bars her door to him and dies of a broken heart. At her grave her lovers meet, and Harford swears eternal revenge.

For the next few years Pulteney wanders about Europe; his romantic plan of effecting an alliance among some Austrian nobles against the tyrannical Emperor results, through Harford's machinations, in his own imprisonment. He escapes of course, but when in Cyprus he triumphs over another hated rival, Prince Menitzen, and marries Helena and they have a child, Harford kidnaps the boy and vows to corrupt him. With Helena dead, Pulteney becomes the pursuer. He is diverted by Prince Menitzen, but he escapes from the Prince's dungeon, rescues an abducted maiden, sees the Prince hanged, and continues his pursuit until in the Appenines, in a storm, he overtakes Harford and the child. He shoots down the keystone of a footbridge with the result that Harford is suspended over a deep ravine. There is a brief battle of wills for the child, then Harford falls and Pulteney enfolds his son to his bosom.

Admittedly the characters are unabashedly flat and the action, through the frequent coincidences and narrow escapes, strains credibility. Yet Henry Pulteney must be commended for its solid structuring of such elements as conflict, motive, suspense, climax, and resolution—in short, its professionalism. The June, 1838, installment, for example, called by the Philadelphia Public Ledger "the gem of Burton's,"[30] contains Helena's rescue:

All looked round as I entered, in amazement at this hostile invasion. When I had reached the central aisle, I sprang from my horse and advanced towards the group, who stood gazing at me in mute surprise.

"Sir priest," said I, calmly and sternly, "in the name of the God at whose altar you serve, I command you to pause ere you wed to this man the wife of another. . . ."

The brother drew his sword. . . . I at once anticipated his intention, and my purpose was formed in a moment. Dashing aside the puny prince who stood trembling in the meanness of guilty cowardice, I seized Helena in my arms, and lifting her into the saddle of the horse, sprung up behind her with the rapidity of light, and turned the animal towards the western end of the church. . . . Almost at one bound my horse cleared the length of the little chapel, and brought me to the door. It swung open, and I perceived to my horror that it gave upon no path or road, but upon a rough ledge of rock which, after descending unevenly for a little distance, terminated abruptly, and presented a steep descent to the sand of the shore below. A glance assured me that a leap would be perilous in the extreme. I looked back and saw lord Angstein rush forward from the door which he had just secured, like the onset of a tiger. I turned to Helena.

"Will you that we remain, or attempt this flight?"

"Fly! oh, fly, at every hazard!"

At the word, I spurred my noble steed forward over the bristling rocks. He clambered safely down the rough declivity, till he reached the edge and looked down upon the depth beneath. He paused as if to summon all the strength of his noble nature, and crouched down till his limbs were almost reclining on the ground. He then gave one lion-like spring, and the air whizzed past my temples with the sound of a rivulet. (2, 397)

In contrast to the high vigor of such a scene, Helena's subsequent death evokes a chanting style reminiscent of Poe in such stories as "Morella" or "Eleonora":

The freshness of health faded gradually from her cheek, and the vigor of her strength declined daily; and the days which she named had not elapsed when she breathed forth her life within my arms. . . . And I took the lifeless form of Helena in my arms, and bore it alone to the spot; and I placed it in the tomb and lifted the huge slab over it. (3, 53)

Praising *Henry Pulteney* for its "energy of style," the *Ledger* praised it also for its "depth of thought." Whether in the form of lyric passages or intellectual discourse, "thought" is a welcome relief here from the concentrated, strenuous action. There is proportionately less of it than in *Stanley*, and the integrated passages—chiefly from the fifth dialogue[31]—are more carefully selected and spaced. The demands of serialization reaped an obvious formalistic benefit here. During one interlude, a perceptive comparison is made between the Mediterranean and Gothic temperaments with reference to art, literature, and religion (2, 91 - 92; *LC*, 277 - 80)—a theme to which Wallace would return in his last essays. During another, Napoleon is severely censured as a ruler. Unlike Tolstoy in *War and Peace*, Wallace accords Napoleon at least military genius, which "raised him to such a height that he was fourteen years in falling to the ground," while France under him "was like a steam-car thrown from its track, and dashing madly through the sand to the nearest precipice" (2, 263; *LC*, 367). But Wallace would have more to say about Napoleon too.

The chief speaker in one of these discussions is Count Mardini, who scorns poetry one moment, reason the next, disparages both Napoleon and democracy, and has a keen eye for the forces of destruction. It is particularly interesting from the vantage point of twentieth-century history to hear the Count say, "Men and nations advance nobly into the illuminated temple of Reform . . . then, as if a demon's eye glared on them, they . . . start back into the darkness and barbarity of threshold times" (2, 264; *LC*, 370). Religious skepticism comes from another speaker, the Englishman Pontarvis: "The universe created God, not God the universe. . . . It is impossible to believe in God without believing wrongly. . . . How can we love . . . or pray to the inconceivable?" Pulteney points to the idolatrous quality of all prayer, which is addressed to "a self-formed idea" rather than God, and Pontarvis concludes by questioning even the practical value of religion as a basis for virtue (4, 288 - 89).

If the bold, often violent physical action in this short novel is a reminder of Clark Hare's observation that Wallace's secret powers were action rather than contemplation, the correspondingly bold, cynical, almost despairing intellectual content makes one feel as though some of the ingredients of Wallace's suicide were caught and held here prophetically. But nothing foreshadows Wallace's own final symptoms as startlingly as Pulteney's state of mind after Lilly's death:

A thousand conflicting passions were battling within my bosom with a vehemence that forbade repose. . . . I felt that I was alone. . . . In sleep, especially, I was harassed, not through the medium of dreams, but by a corporeal sense of nervous oppression, which often startled me from slumber, with a momentary belief that madness was upon me. (2, 89)

V *Short Fiction*

Wallace's first known story, "Confessions of a Dreamer,"[32] previously noted biographically, warrants a second look here. In its overall ironic fantasy it shows the effect of Washington Irving's *Sketchbook*, but precisely in the autobiographical sense already noted, it has a depth all its own. "From earliest youth I have been a dreamer," says the narrator at the outset, "a dreamer by day and a dreamer by night," and for the next few sentences one seems to be in the land not of Irving but of Poe, in whose works the dream in its various forms figures so largely. The narrator in Wallace's story can even shape his dreams by making them a continuation of his waking thoughts, so that his subsequent vision of the Temple of Oblivion becomes all the more conscious and prophetic. The story gathers force as the dreamer contemplates "the glories of the Forgotten Past"—heroes and poets confident of being remembered; the architect of the Pyramids—but also the unknown and unexpected—"the virtues of Nero, the vices of Alfred"—until at last, horrified, he sees the book containing his own writings.

In "An Incident at La Trappe," which appeared in the *New York Mirror* almost a year later,[33] a dying monk who left a "much-loved brother, involved in a whirlpool of dissipation and sin," discovers that the monk living in the next cell is he. The old monk dies, saying, "In silence we have worked out our salvation upon earth; but we *will* speak, my dear brother! we will speak in heaven!" In its brevity, poignancy, and other-worldly aspect this piece is as much a parable as a story, and once again the autobiographical element is unmistakable in the brothers' living in silence and isolation not only from the world but also from each other. Did Wallace see his brother John in the "good" monk and himself in the "sinner"? His eventual suicide would lead one to think so.

Wallace's remaining eight stories, most of which appeared in *Godey's Lady's Book*, are as one might expect, less literary and bear a higher degree of professional polish. Their theme is love. Of this group the earliest one, "The Victims of Passion,"[34] is perhaps the most interesting, since it is a study in the destructive, rather than constructive, power of love. Godari, the protagonist, is a young Indian priest in love with the beautiful Chatrya; but since she loves King Goroyen, Godari proceeds to ruin the pair. Not content with having driven Chatrya to destitution, Godari plots the death of King Goroyen and his Queen, Godari's own sister, in order to gain the throne. Chatrya intervenes, sending herself and Godari instead to their graves. Since the setting is India, Wallace could afford to interject a degree of sexual frankness that is unusual in the period, especially in stories appearing in *Godey's*. In one scene, after young King Goroyen has rescued Chatrya from a wild boar, he is permitted a glimpse at "the exquisite fairness of her bosom." The reader is told subsequently that they become lovers, and she bears an illegitimate child (pp. 128 - 29). In Godari, who became a priest because of his "refined selfishness," rather than "through sacrifice," one is reminded somewhat of Tyler. But Godari is young, and his evil doing is more passionate than calculated. He is one of those people whose "sensitivity makes them miserable, and their misery makes them wicked. . . . They dwell ceaselessly on self; for what indeed is genius, but intense mental selfishness? They desire not to love but to be loved." Interestingly, among the early influences on Godari was an elder brother who was "cold, callous, and unfeeling" and "took a savage pleasure in tyrannizing over the tenderness of his brother" (p. 125).

"The Tyrolean Lovers,"[35] as well as the stories that follow, ends happily. The general formula is the overcoming of some obstacle to love, such as pride or poverty or jealousy. Here, the obstacle is a pre-arranged marriage—as it turns out, between an already loving pair. Wallace carries off the old plot trick with a degree of charm, the fairy-tale ingenuousness of the situation matching the youth and simplicity of the characters and the purity of the Alpine setting.

With "Pride and Love"[36] we move into the American upper class. Miss Vassal, who has received some love poems from Edward Clavering, believes that his request that she keep them private comes from "a wish to draw back from the position which he had there taken." When she reads them again, however, her more generous feelings gain ascendancy and she becomes convinced that Clavering means the passion his poems express. But now he is in her power, and "the pleasure of punishing a lover is a temptation irresistible to women" (p. 229).

"The Lover and the Poet"[37] again approaches the fairy tale, since the obstacle is Miss Percival's ignorance that an anonymous poet—who seems to speak to her directly—and her suitor Merivale are the same person. But Merivale's characterization is worth noting. An anonymous author, "the slave of a host of passions," whose only real satisfaction comes from creative work, he has acquired his immense learning against the grain. "Constitutionally

impulsive . . . he hated learning; and because he hated, he would
subdue and possess it" (p. 257).

"The Course of Love"[38] gives a good illustration of the
shallowness of some of these formula stories. The obstacle here is
Miss Stuart's jealousy. Her lover, Walter Egerton, has "the rapid,
intense fancy of the poet" that enables him to fall in love with a
pretty face in an instant, "till the effacing influence of the days
wore down the impression" (pp. 130 - 131); and to make matters
worse, Egerton's vanity makes him affect an air of licentiousness.
When it becomes clear that he is fundamentally decent and has not
"one recollection of purity destroyed," Miss Stuart, who lives by
the formula that appearances deceive, is made happy.

As though growing weary of these stories, Wallace permitted intellectual discussion to take up nearly half of the next one, "The
Head and the Heart." Possibly because it was intended for the
more sophisticated *Graham's Magazine*,[39] the narrative, too, moves
on a somewhat higher level. The protagonist is the eccentric com-
poser, Mr. Nivernois, who is too busy lecturing to Miss Stanhope
about Napoleon and Wellington to realize that he loves her. Even
after falling in love with her portrait at a gallery, he has some trouble associating the picture with the girl. The comic element in the
situation is enhanced by Nivernois's mad behavior, such as his
stealing an unpurchasable painting or rushing into a strange drawing room to play the piano. Once again this story exhibits that interesting counter-movement in values which characterizes some of
the dialogue in *Henry Pulteney*. "No lasting fame can be founded
on music," says Nivernois sitting in a box at the opera and interfer-
ing with the playing of his own music. "No melody is immortal but
that of the drum and the canon. . . . How the Corsican knew to
touch that instrument" (p. 20). In a more earnest tone, Nivernois
speaks of the largeness, complexity, and shifting quality of
Napoleon's soul. Wellington, who did not have Napoleon's genius
but emerged the greater man through effort, was an expression of
England with her "integrity, good sense, and solid freedom," as
Napoleon was of France, "which has no power save of paroxysms,
and cannot cease to be frivolous but by becoming ferocious."
Wallace is not averse to carrying the comparison to its conclusion
by likening Wellington to a Tartar horseman "with one perpetual
posture," and Napoleon to an agile "monkey on a circus horse"
(pp. 21 - 22).

As Nivernois finds Napoleon's soul large, so Clarendon, the hero of "The Triumph of Love"[40] finds it small. Only Napoleon's fertile, forceful intellect and "his untamed, tireless energy" are praised here, so that "since his career, there is no excuse for dullness or idleness" (p. 161). Clarendon, incidentally, is a remarkably erudite, brave, and handsome man, whose only fault is that he is poor. Consequently he is in some ways too proud, but when he "inherits" money from an unknown source his excess pride dissolves. When he discovers that the source of the money is his beloved Miss Paulet, the reader expects something terrible, but love triumphs.

Wallace's last known story, "The Masquerade,"[41] introduces a villain as the obstacle to love. He is Mary Temple's impoverished cousin, who hopes through marriage with her to regain some of his fortune. One night he waylays her and tries to force her to marry him before a presumably false priest, but the heroic Edward Carlton rescues her and challenges Temple to a duel. Postponing the combat, Temple plots Carlson's death but is killed by a runaway horse and, dying, repents. The flatness of the characterization fails to lift this story from melodrama, but it is told with economy; and the masked ball, where Mary and Carlton meet, the moonlit beach before the ancestral mansion, and Mary's visionary appearance before Carlton are convincing atmospheric elements.

With "The Masquerade" Wallace, to all appearances, gave up the writing of fiction, which is not surprising. If we extracted the intellectual content that he consciously put into his love stories, they would remain thin. He could provide physical suspense in his adventure fiction and a definable inner conflict in his sentimental fiction that made them welcome to the magazines. But his keenest psychological observations, like his ideas in general, remain outside. It seems as though after his first literary attempts Wallace stopped trusting fiction with his whole creative intellect, so that technique remained for him mere trickery, which he with his searching mind soon grew tired of. In terms of Coleridge's important critical distinction current at the time, Wallace's approach to his later fiction was not truly imaginative, only fanciful.

VI *Aphorisms and "Monologues"*

The remaining non-fiction pieces that comprise Wallace's first period are his aphorisms and his series called "Monologues among the Mountains." The aphorisms appeared in *Burton's Gentleman's*

Magazine as three sets of "Sweepings from a Drawer" in 1839,[42] and three sets of "Mems for Memory" in 1840.[43] There are nearly one hundred and fifty of them; some are sufficiently sharp to be called epigrams, some offer practical advice in the form of maxims, a few are extended into miniature essays. Wallace's interest in brief, pithy sayings seems to stem from his reading of the Greek and Roman classics; the genre was also in favor during the eighteenth century. The Romantic impulse in much of Wallace's writing seems here to seek its own rigid control. The passions, for example, are again and again disparaged; at one point they are "the dung about the roots of the powers, by which they are nourished into luxuriance and size" (4, 241). Wallace's open, searching mind is everywhere perceptible, as he probes the nature of God, evil, morals, politics, manners, or the human situation. He can be cynical: "Men worship most the man that worships least" (5, 236); but also hopeful, likening the discoveries of genius to sailing upstream into an unexplored country: "Every thing that is near flies backward from thee, and thou goest unattended and alone. But look above thee, and look beyond, and the heavens, and the distant parts of the earth, are moving onward with thee" (5, 236). Some of these aphorisms in the "Mems for Memory" sets impressed Poe so favorably that he copied them into his "Marginalia"; but for the present-day reader the genre is archaic, and the verbal concentration does not always pay off in corresponding poignance.

No such formal control hampers "Monologues among the Mountains,"[44] whose biographical interest has been noted. The human situation is presented here in terms of largeness and openness—in giving free rein to passion, love, possession, power. The world of men is confining; hence the Cosmopolite lives alone among the mountains. Another Tyler-like figure in his taste for and range of experience, except moving within the limits of morality, he has already fought out the mortal battle between the world, "which is Time's eldest champion," and the soul, "which is the youngest offspring of Eternity," and has emerged victorious. Now he is old, and flinging from him "the powerless foe," he goes forth calm, strong, and confident into the realm of thought.

He is also "thrown high upon the beach," where he "lies amid the wrecks and rubbish of old and ruined schemes" (*LC*, 422), giving a less distinct impression of victory. But consistency or systematic thought is not the forte of these "rhapsodies." Rather they are a quest for beauty, wherever thought and feeling range;

and the paltriness of man is as freely reckoned with as in the aphorisms. But "grief of heart is the quickening spell of the mind's inspiration; and the ruin of the individual is the glory of the race" (*LC*, 408).

In the second essay, thought settles into a specific aesthetic. After a hymn to the sun, comes the Platonic assertion: "There is in Life an idea above Life." This idea is beauty, "and the mean of its realization is art." The ideal is a perfection of the actual, but it differs from it in essence. This essence is form. Besides "the beauty of material form," which we seek through what we conventionally call art, there are other types of beauty we seek through our various faculties. Thus, the art of science leads to the beauty of intellectual form, the art of religion to goodness, philosophy to virtue, politics to society, and among some "rare souls" mathematics to the "abstract beauty of mathematical forms." To seek beauty in its various forms is the purpose of man's existence (*LC*, 414 - 15).

This elevation of beauty among the supposedly "equal" Platonic values gives an important insight into Wallace's inner world underneath his daily thirteen hours of investigating trust titles (*LC*, 399). In the third essay, he lets the whole elaborate structure go in order to assert it in more conventional terms: "Art is greater than science; for to create is more than to know" (*LC*, 419). He goes on to say that "the true seat of creative vigor is the sentiments," which are "blended of passion and intelligence." The sentiments are three-fold: natural, spiritual, and moral; therefore art, too, may be natural as among the Greeks, spiritual as among the Hebrews, and moral as among the Romans (*LC*, 425). The fourth essay attempts to apply this principle to English poetry: Chaucer is a Greek poet, Milton a Hebrew poet, and Pope a Roman poet. Shakespeare is too great to fit into any scheme; but in Spenser, "the spiritual, the moral, and the natural combine in the most exquisite justness of proportion" (*LC*, 434 - 38). Wallace would continue such cultural-aesthetic speculations in future writings; meanwhile the fragmentary character of this fourth essay kept it confined to his notebook. The elaborate prefatory characterization of the speaker in "To the Reader" was also omitted when the first three essays appeared in *Graham's Magazine* in 1845 and 1846. They are simply and enigmatically signed, "A Cosmopolite."

CHAPTER 3

Poe, Griswold, and Wallace

I *Tyler, Dupin, and Others*

EDGAR Allan Poe came to Philadelphia in the summer of
1838,[1] when "William Landor" was making his debut in the
magazines and *Stanley* was about to appear and win high acclaim.
In Poe's career, 1838 was a difficult year. Eleven years had passed
since his first publication, *Tamerlane and Other Poems*, and he had
eleven more years to live. He had done some of his best writing,
and he had had his first success as editor of the *Southern Literary
Messenger;* but he was now jobless, and he had hit a creative
plateau. The pinnacle of success in the editorial chair of *Graham's
Magazine*, as well as the writing of most of his greatest works, was
still before him.

When Poe read *Stanley*—probably late in 1838 or early in
1839—he had written "Ligeia," but was yet to write "The Fall of
the House of Usher," "William Wilson," and his tales of ratiocination. That he read at least parts of *Stanley* with greater intensity
than he read any other book is shown by the twenty-odd separate
passages in his subsequent writings that he borrowed from
Stanley.[2] Before turning to these, one might try to account for
Poe's unusual interest in this book.

The author of "Tamerlane" was no doubt struck, first of all, by
the anatomy of ambition as it appears in *Stanley*. In Poe's poem
world conquest is not presented as immoral, but it does betray
love:

> I spoke to her of power and pride,
> But mystically—in such guise
> That she might deem it nought beside
> The moment's converse. . . .

Tyler too was a lover before he renounced human feeling and embraced ambition. If Tamerlane's is a projection of Poe's own artistic ambition, young Stanley's course of study and writing provides an even closer parallel. After Emily's cool reception, Stanley resolves that "ambition . . . should feel no defeat" (I, 35). As Tamerlane says, "passion must, with youth, expire." Poe might even have suspected that *Stanley* was influenced by "Tamerlane," which had by then appeared three times, in 1827, 1829, and 1831, but both poem and novel are so heavily saturated with Byronism that direct influence is not an inevitable conclusion. Poe, at any rate, did not cry plagiarism.

If Poe was little edified by the moral contrast between Stanley and Tyler, the two characters as psychological counterparts doubtless interested the author of "Morella" and "Ligeia," who would go on experimenting with two further types of psychic interrelation in "The Fall of the House of Usher" (1839) and "William Wilson" (1839). Both of these stories suggest the influence of *Stanley.* The narrative strategy in "The Fall of the House of Usher" is similar to that in the final portion of the novel.[3] The letter summoning the narrator, the solitary ride on horseback through a wild country, the reception by the ailing host in his mansion generate a similar atmosphere also. Usher is a friend, whereas Tyler is an enemy, but both men are similarly ravaged by a malady that is more psychological than physical. Roderick Usher's solitary dreaming—diseased yet devoted to art—into which the narrator has been drawn "for many solemn hours" is reminiscent of yet another episode in the novel, in which Stanley visits Mr. Thirlwall (II, 101 - 13). Living in his ivy-covered Tudor mansion Thirlwall is portrayed as a dreamer. In some moments he would exhibit a nervousness, in others he would fall into a revery, "film would gather over his eye," and he would begin to ramble or altogether cease talking. Unfit for the world and therefore contemptuous of it, he lives among his books, "his brow . . . furrowed with premature wrinkles, and his countenance . . . care-worn and jaded." "I look upon myself as having discovered the art of life," Thirlwall says at one point, foreshadowing Huysmans, who in turn would acknowledge the great influence on him of Poe.[4]

The similarity between "William Wilson" and *Stanley* is both thematic and structural. The two Wilsons might be thought of as psychological counterparts, such as Stanley and Tyler, extended into Doppelgänger oneness. In both works, a life of crime is recounted in the first person. "Death approaches," says William Wilson at the beginning of the story, "and the shadow which foreruns him has thrown a softening influence over my spirit." Tyler, making his death-bed confession in the last portion of the novel, is similarly softened. The moral direction of the theme, which is unusual for Poe, the realistic setting, and the cosmopolitan range bring the two works still closer.

More specific is the effect of *Stanley* on Poe's tales of ratiocination, where some of the borrowed passages may be found. The narrator in "The Murders in the Rue Morgue" (1841) says of Poe's detective hero, C. Auguste Dupin: "He boasted to me, with a low chuckling laugh, that most men in respect to himself, wore windows in their bosoms" (*Works*, IV, 152). Correspondingly, Tyler speaks of those with whom he dealt: "Their bosom was windowed to my view" (II, 242). The fact that Dupin is a useful citizen and Tyler a criminal fades in the light of their both being conceived largely in terms of dream and intellect.[5] If one general statement can be made about all of Poe's writings, it is that—whether enticingly or jejunely—they show an intellectual ingredient mixed into the dream. Poe saw this same mixture in *Stanley*, with the intellectual element somewhat predominating. It was just what Poe, a born dreamer, wanted from this novel. He, who in his semi-fictitious "Philosophy of Composition" would attempt to reduce the creation of his "Raven" into a complex formula, must have been delighted to hear one of the dinner guests say in the second dialogue, "I do not yet despair of seeing the formula of a temple or an overture" (I, 109; *LC*, 270). But to return to "The Murders in the Rue Morgue": it has been said that it takes a thief to catch a thief, and it is quite possible that Poe's initial idea for Dupin—and with him, the tale of ratiocination—comes from Tyler, who eliminated feeling in order to allow the greater ascendancy of the intellect, which would make him a master criminal. This connection would give Wallace a seat at the fountainhead of the detective story—just a little left of Poe.

The passage from *Stanley* occurring in Poe's "Mystery of Marie Rogêt" (1842 - 43) is not a borrowing but a footnote attributed to "Landor" (causing millions of future readers to think that Poe had Walter Savage Landor in mind). Beginning rather abstrusely, the passage leads up to the statement that "when law becomes a science and a system, it ceases to be justice" and is occasioned by

Dupin's observation that "very much of what is rejected as evidence by a court, is the best evidence to the intellect."[6]

Similarly critical is Dupin, in "The Purloined Letter," of the Prefect's methods of crime detection. By way of illustration, he quotes the account of a boy who could read minds: "I fashion the expression of my face, as accurately as possible, in accordance with the expression of his, and then wait to see what thoughts or sentiments arise in my mind or heart" (*Works*, VI, 41). In *Stanley*, Tyler cites Campanella (also mentioned by Dupin): "When he wished to discover the leading characteristics of any one whom he saw, he arranged his features into a similitude with theirs and observed what emotions rose within his heart" (II, 242 - 43).

The same story gives us what is perhaps Poe's most interesting borrowing from Wallace: Tyler's challenging criticism of mathematics as a system of general truth. Whether Poe received his ideas about the philosophical limitations of mathematics originally from *Stanley* is not certain. But they occur noticeably in his writings after his reading of *Stanley*, specifically in his stories of ratiocination and finally in *Eureka*, where Newton and Laplace are said to be limited metaphysically because they were "mathematicians solely" (*Works*, XVI, 223). Moreover, whether for the first time or not, he found in *Stanley* these ideas so clearly articulated that he partly paraphrased, partly copied them in his "Purloined Letter."

Tyler says: "The axioms of mathematics are not axioms of general truth; they are derived from the consideration of form and quantity, and it does not follow that what is true of form and quantity is true of moral principles or of human motives." Dupin says: "The mathematics are the science of form and quantity. . . . Mathematical axioms are not axioms of general truth. What is true of relation—of form and quantity—is often grossly false in regard to morals, for example."

Tyler says further, "Another mathematical axiom which is not true in the general reason is, that all the parts taken together are equal to the whole. This is not always true of physical science, and is generally false in morals. It is not true in chymical [sic] combinations." Dupin says further: "In [morals] it is very usually untrue that the aggregated parts are equal to the whole. In chemistry also the axiom fails."

Tyler says further, "I might name to you many other principles of mathematical science which are not true beyond the boundaries of that science." Dupin says, "There are numerous other mathematical truths which are only truths within the limits of relation."[7]

Sometimes Poe was chiefly interested in borrowing a striking metaphor or allusion. Just before he dies, Tyler says: "It is with me as if a voyager of a desert should raise his eyes and be assured that there was no vulture nigh, while the beak of the monster was fastened in his heart" (II, 251 - 52). In "The Raven" the half line, "Take thy beak from out my heart," depicts a similar type of suffering, making the bird "emblematical," as Poe himself explains in his "Philosophy of Composition," of "mournful and never-ending remembrance" (*Works*, XIV, 208). Poe's "Premature Burial" has a borrowed passage depicting Afrasiab sailing down the Oxus in the company of sleeping demons. Only, whereas in *Stanley* it is the passions that, like the demons, must not be awakened or we are lost (I, 124; *LC*, 289), in Poe's tale it is "the grim legions of sepulchral terrors" (*Works*, V, 273; XVI, 167). The long series of borrowings in Poe's "Marginalia," which will be more convenient to examine later, are similar in scope.

Sometimes Poe was more interested in ideas. In the third dialogue in *Stanley*, after Mr. Woodward's anti-democratic tirade, the narrator associates the rise of crime with the rise of knowledge. In Poe's "Colloquy of Monos and Una" (1841), Monos says, "Wild attempts at an omni-prevalent Democracy were made. Yet this evil sprang necessarily from the leading evil—Knowledge" (*Works*, IV, 203). Subsequently Monos laments: "Alas, for the μουσική which [Plato] justly regarded as an all sufficient education for the soul." A footnote discussing the extended meaning of μουσική among the Greeks corresponds to a similar discussion of "music" in the second dialogue in *Stanley* (I, 108 - 9; *LC*, 269 - 70). Earlier in that dialogue it is asserted that metaphysically the senses are one (I, 108; *LC*, 269). In Poe's work, after Monos had died his senses were "assuming often each other's functions at random" (*Works*, IV, 206).

These dialogues in *Stanley* may, incidentally, have had an effect on Poe's casting "Monos and Una," as well as its preceding and following companion pieces, "The Conversation of Eiros and Charmion" (1839) and "The Power of Words" (1845), in dialogue form also. Dungeon scenes are fairly common in this period, but the multiplication of torture in "The Pit and the Pendulum" (1843) is reminiscent of a scene in *Stanley* in which a prisoner dying of thirst is given poisoned water to drink (II, 195 - 97). We can make an imaginative connection between Mr. Thirlwall in *Stanley* and the protagonist in Poe's "Man of the Crowd" (1840), who after a lifetime of solitary dreaming makes a desperate and futile attempt to mingle with the crowds. If we accept an allegorical reading of "The Masque of the Red Death" (1842), whereby Prince Prospero's castle—in the manner of Usher's house—is a head with its faculties barred from other vital functions (the seven colors perhaps groping toward some scheme of sensation such as Rimbaud's theory of vowels), the final "illimitable dominion" of the Red Death might be another expression of the doom upon Tyler, who has isolated his mind from human feeling.

More specific was Poe's interest in the numerous passages of literary criticism in *Stanley*. Poe, who had by this time shown himself in some ways to be a disciple of Coleridge and denounced what he called Wordsworth's didacticism, had little critical theory to learn from the kind of rambling, semi-biographical discourse about authors that fills the pages of *Stanley*. Yet he read them with special care, turning to them for many of his borrowings and in one instance, as will be seen, consulting "Landor" as an expert littérateur.

For, although a rather consistent theory can be extracted from the totality of Poe's critical writings, an attempt to fit all of these into a system is to twist Poe somewhat out of shape. Poe was not a systematic thinker but a spontaneous, highly imaginative writer with a strong accompanying taste for the rational—a classic rationalizer, in Freudian jargon. In his "Letter to B—" (1831), for example, his scorn for Wordsworth is probably a result less of Wordsworth's didacticism than of his simplicism in such poems as "The Idiot Boy" or "The Pet Lamb."

Nine years later, having warmed up to Wordsworth—a process in which *Stanley* probably played a part—Poe was able to write that Wordsworth, like Aristotle, "has reference to instruction with eternity in view" (*Works*, XI, 12). Whereas *Stanley* was unable to change the cool respect in which Poe held Pope, the novel seems to have struck a sympathetic chord in him with respect to Byron. Both Poe and Wallace were under Byron's irresistible spell, both fighting it yet succumbing to it. The evidence is clearly in *Stanley*. Poe, similarly, never misses an opportunity to point out Byron's defects in versification; then suddenly in 1844—in a mood that harks back to "The Assignation" ten years previously—he holds forth on Byron's ethereal love for Mary Chaworth, letting slip that the real reason for his recent disparagement was not Byron's versification but "the gross earthliness pervading and disfiguring his ordinary love poems" (*Works*, XIV, 150). In the course of his random comments on Byron, Poe wrote to James Russell Lowell in 1843 that Byron "was no artist";[8] in *Stanley*, we recall, one speaker asserts in the fourth dialogue that Byron "wrote true poetry without being a poet."

Shelley, the same speaker continues, was by contrast "born a bard." Poe wrote in 1845 that Shelley had sung "as the bird sings—impulsively—earnestly—with utter abandonment—to himself solely," adding: "His rhapsodies are but the rough notes—the stenographic memoranda of poems" (*Works*, XII, 32). Earlier in the same dialogue in *Stanley*, Shelley's works are held to be "not so much poems as splendid storehouses of poetical materials" (II, 80; *LC*, 339).

Coleridge's influence on Poe was too intricate from the outset to be affected by the essentially non-theoretical discussions in *Stanley*. It is nevertheless noteworthy that it was only after reading the novel that Poe expressed himself specifically on Coleridge's famous distinction between imagination and fancy. Up to 1838 Poe had been simply accepting "imagination" in Coleridge's sense, defining it as the creative power in man" (*Works*, VIII, 283). Then in 1840 he took issue with Coleridge, denying that "the fancy combines" and "the imagination creates." There is not between the two "even a difference of *degree*. The fancy as nearly creates as the imagination; and neither creates in any respect. All novel conceptions are merely unusual combinations" (*Works*, X, 61 - 62). It may be that Poe received a cue from Milton as he is quoted in *Stanley*: "A poem is . . . created by the imagination, by combining, with taste and judgment, ingredients selected from the stores of fancy" (I, 54; *LC*, 255).

The one author who is treated savagely in *Stanley* is Bulwer. Possibly, as has been suggested,[9] the underlying motive for much American disparagement of Bulwer was Victorian prudery; still, whereas prior to reading *Stanley* Poe had been Bulwer's outspoken defender, saying that he was "unsurpassed by any writer living or dead" (*Works*, VIII, 223), early in 1839, while reading or having just read *Stanley*, he blasted Bulwer for his tendency to "ape the externals of deep meaning," for his "senseless mannerisms," and for his attempts to pass off "abominable rigmarole" as philosophy (*Works*, XIV, 91 - 92). These comments were but a prelude to a more systematic and detailed destruction of Bulwer that Poe was to execute two years later in his review of Bulwer's *Night and Morning* (*Works*, X, 114 - 33)—an important statement, incidentally, on the novel. After that Poe was free to read Bulwer again "with the highest pleasure," though remembering that "Mr. Bulwer is never lucid, and seldom profound" (*Works*, X, 212).

II *Poe and "Landor"*

Poe served as editor of *Burton's Gentleman's Magazine* from July, 1839, to June, 1840, and of *Graham's Magazine* from April, 1841, to May, 1842, and in that capacity bought works from "William Landor" and corresponded with him. In the one extant letter between them dated July 7, 1841 (which, however, implies several additional ones), Poe apologizes for not having answered an inquiry by "Landor" sooner. He adds in a postscript,

You have seen, I believe, the July no: of Mag. Among the critical notices is one on Bolingbroke, the only notice not written by myself. There are passages in that critique which I am sure are *stolen*, although I cannot put my hand upon the original. Your acquaintance with Bolingbroke's commentators is more extensive than my own. Can you aid me in tracing the theft? I am anxious to do so. Has not Bulwer written something like it?[10]

Here Poe is making an obvious reference to *Stanley*—without any self-consciousness. Even more interesting is the fact that in view of the borrowed passage in "The Murders in the Rue Morgue," which came out in the April issue of *Graham's*, Poe should be trying three months later to enlist "Landor" in his detective work to uncover plagiarism.

Publicly, Poe made the association between *Stanley* and "Landor" four months later, in "A Chapter on Autography," as previously noted. Poe's next reference to "Landor" involved Nathaniel P. Willis, who had been attacked through 1843 by some of the British reviews. Wallace rose to Willis's defense in a sketch published in *Graham's* in April, 1844, in "Our Contributors" series.[11] It was signed "L." Poe wrote to James R. Lowell on March 30, 1844: "I presume you have read the Memoir of Willis, in the April No: of G. It is written by a Mr Landor—but I think it full of hyperbole. Willis is no genius—a graceful trifler—no more."[12] Poe was right of course; the *Graham's* article is obvious puffery, and Wallace was to reverse his position sharply on Willis later. But Poe,

who within a few months would be employed by Willis and George
P. Morris on their *Evening Mirror*, was struggling between critical
conscience and prudence, and the "Landor" article kept preying
on his mind. Writing from New York to the *Columbia Spy*, he
made references to it in Letters VI (June 18, 1844) and VII (June
25),[13] sometimes agreeing, sometimes disagreeing, struggling apparently not only with Willis but with "Landor" also.

Exactly a year after his article on Willis, Wallace published one
on George P. Morris, in *Graham's*, signed once more "L."[14] His
motives were again altruistic, this time with a strong intermixture
of personal friendship. Morris, we recall, was having financial dif-
ficulties at this time, and many of his friends were coming to his
aid. Poe, writing in the *Broadway Journal*, was once again ambivalent toward "L," calling the Morris sketch "the most interesting feature" of the *Graham's* number, yet blaming it for excess praise.[15]

Meanwhile the famous Longfellow war had flared into full blaze.
It had begun in January, when in the pages of the *Evening Mirror*
Poe reviewed Longfellow's *Waif* and made a subtle imputation
against Longfellow's literary honesty.[16] There was an answer and a
renewed charge, but the matter simmered on for eight weeks until
an anonymous correspondent "Outis" (who may have been Poe
himself) attacked Poe in the *Evening Mirror* on March 8, 1845, via
"The Raven" for his excessive preoccupation with plagiarism. Poe,
who had just become coeditor of the *Broadway Journal*, replied in
that publication through five weekly articles, "proving" Longfellow a plagiarist.[17]

Wallace's anonymous article, "Plagiarism," appeared in the
National Press almost a year later, on March 14, 1846. It is possible
that he had sent it to Morris considerably earlier; on the other
hand, it was his habit as controversialist to let his opponent exhaust
himself before he delivered his dictum from on high. The tone of
the opening paragraph is certainly in accord with such a strategy:

The literary community was, of late, extensively disturbed by an alarm on
the subject of *plagiarism*. Startled by the suggestions of an acute and ardent critic—one whose eccentricities always attract by their brilliancy and
whose greatest errors seem but the excesses of a too subtle understanding—the public had become wellnigh worried into a panic of
terror. . . . With an ingenuity of fearlessness, as singular as it was mistaken, this critical agitation set chiefly against an Eastern bard.

. . . Meanwhile, the public, which in its quiet way, detects a false alarm as speedily as it does a real imposture, has gone on reading and enjoying Mr. Longfellow and his suspected brethren, much in the spirit of Charles the Second, who, when he was told that all of Dryden's plays were stolen, answered, that he wished that those who said so would steal him as good plays as Dryden's. For our own part, we have always met these charges of plagiarism, when put forth in an uncandid and hostile spirit, with a blank and absolute incredulity. We refuse even to listen to them, regarding them as founded in complete error and misconception. (*ASE*, 433)

In the second paragraph, Wallace states his thesis, which corresponds to Poe's own more sober thoughts on the subject. "This tendency to plagiarize," says Wallace, "is a certain and almost inseparable characteristic of the poetic faculty." For, as Poe stated in the April 5, 1845, issue of the *Broadway Journal:* "The poetic sentiment . . . implies . . . an abnormally keen appreciation of the beautiful, with a longing for its assimilation, or absorption, into the poetic identity. What a poet intensely admires, becomes thus, in very fact, although only partially, a portion of his own intellect" (*Works*, XII, 105). Originality is of secondary importance. Whereas Poe seems at best to excuse plagiarism, Wallace, using the theory of combination, asserts that "the partial or imperfect conceptions of others form as lawful a subject for the amending and exalting exertions of the poet, as the natural objects or relations which those conceptions concern" (*ASE*, 435). But Wallace makes a distinction: "A cold and lifeless transcription from the writings of another, is, of course, a wholly distinct affair. That is a question not of inference, but of evidence: it is an imposture, which, when once discovered, stands exposed forever" (*ASE*, 434).

Was Wallace here reprimanding Poe himself? If he had read the November, 1844, issue of the *Democratic Review* and the September, 1845, issue of *Godey's Lady's Book*, he was aware that Poe had committed just such "cold and lifeless transcription" in four instances in his "Marginalia" series from *Stanley*. For the "Marginalia" consists of paragraph-long essays, each independent from the next, and there can be little application of "absorption into the poetic identity." If you stole one, you stole a unit.

If one of Poe's motives in his lifelong concern with plagiarism was to display his knowledge of literature, Wallace makes his own dazzling display in the remainder of his article. Quoting several passages, especially from Byron, he shows echoes of Dryden, Pope, Burns, Bacon, and others. In his concluding paragraph he states sternly,

We have a very strong feeling on the subject of these charges of plagiarism. We deprecate such imputations as in the highest degree mischievous. They are not merely unjust, in making an individual responsible for what is a professional characteristic; but they are eminently injurious to Art, by diffusing the notion that originality is the first excellence in poetry, whereas beauty is its only legitimate search. . . . Those from whom these charges proceed, show an ignorance of the distinctions and limits of the different departments of human intelligence in regard to orginality. (*ASE*, 440)

In answer—if one takes his comments in "The Literati" installment in the July, 1846, issue of *Godey's* as such—Poe stresses that plagiarism does not necessarily involve any "moral delinquency" and repeats that "the poetic sentiment presupposes a keen appreciation of the beautiful with a longing for its assimilation into the poetic identity." As in the previous article, Poe points out that within the borrower's soul the borrowed material "has a secondary origination; and the poet, thus possessed by another's thought, cannot be said to take of it possession. But in either view he thoroughly feels it as *his own*." He admits once again: "For the most frequent and palpable plagiarisms we must search the works of the most eminent poets" (*Works*, XV, 62 - 63).

What may be taken to be Wallace's answer is contained in his review of Poe's *Raven and Other Poems* in the October 10 issue of the *National Press*. Wallace begins by bestowing high praise on Poe's fiction: "Narratives which rivet the interest, and sway the passions as powerfully as his do, indicate a vigor of imagination that might send its productions forward far along the line of future life. Many of his tales, we have no doubt, will long survive, as among the ablest and most remarkable of American productions" (*LC*, 37). But there is something strained, unfelt, grudging in these words; Wallace has written better criticism. He seems to be more comfortable as he reprimands Poe for quarreling:

To one who possesses the powers of close, logical reasoning, and of pointed and piercing sarcasm, the "*torva voluptas*" of literary and social controversy is often a fatal fascination. But a man who is conscious within himself of faculties which indicate to him that he was born, not to wrangle with the men of his own times, but to speak truth and peace to distant ages and remote posterity, ought to make a covenant with himself, that he will be drawn aside by no temptation.

The second part of the reprimand is more subtle:

As an analytical critic, Mr. Poe possesses abilities quite unrivalled in this country, and perhaps on either side of the water. We have scarcely ever taken up one of his more careful critical papers, on some author or work worthy of his strength, without a sense of surprise at the novel and profound views from which his inquiries began, nor followed their development without the closest interest, nor laid the essay down without admiration and respect for the masculine and acute understanding with which we had coped during the perusal. But in the case of inventive genius so brilliant and vigorous as is shown in his poems, and in the papers to which we have alluded, we feel that even criticism of the highest kind is an employment below the true measure of its dignity, and, we may say, its duty; for to be a tender of the light in another man's tomb, is no fit occupation for one who is able to kindle a lamp of his own, whose ray may abide against all the force of the night, and storms, and time. The poet's is a consecrating gift. A man who can produce such a work as "The Raven," ought to feel that it was his office to afford subjects, and not models, to criticism. (*LC*, 37 - 38)

The patronizing tone is unmistakable, as is the conscious restraint. And Wallace appears elsewhere to have a perfectly sound respect for criticism!

It would be dramatic to be able to write that Poe in answer stole twenty-six more items from Wallace. But, although he did just that, there is no way of knowing whether, even if he read these comments, he knew that they came from "Landor." Neither the review, nor the preceding article on plagiarism was signed, and one cannot rely on the claim Poe made earlier that he could recognize "Landor's" style.[18]

It is impossible to know, for example, whether, if Poe read the "Cosmopolite's" effusions in *Graham's*, he recognized the identity behind that pseudonym. In any case, what is expressed there about beauty as "an idea above life" is also expressed in a central passage in Poe's "Poetic Principle" (1850) with striking similarity. Wallace wrote,

There is in life an idea above Life. The being of man is infected with the apprehension of a state and character of existence beyond the experience

of his daily consciousness. Toward this condition, his nature is stung by a
perpetual and inherent uneasiness; and in it alone it rests. This Life above
Life is Beauty; and the mean of its realization is Art. (*LC*, 414 - 15)

Poe's passage may or may not show direct influence. But it does
show a remarkable kinship with Wallace's mind:

An immortal instinct, deep within the spirit of man, is thus, plainly, a
sense of the Beautiful. . . . This thirst belongs to the immortality of Man.
It is at once a consequence and an indication of his perennial existence. It
is the desire of the moth for the star. It is no mere appreciation of the
Beauty before us—but a wild effort to reach the Beauty above. (*Works*,
XIV, 273)

As for those twenty-six additonal "cold and lifeless transcrip-
tions," they appeared in further installments of Poe's "Marginalia," in the May, June, and July, 1849, issues of the *Southern
Literary Messenger*. The source for them is *Stanley* and
Wallace's "Mems for Memory" series in *Burton's*, all three installments incuded in volume seven of the bound magazine. That
Poe should have these books with him at this time is notable in
view of the fact that when he came to New York in the spring of
1845, he and his wife Virginia had left her mother, Mrs. Clemm,
behind in Philadelphia to sell some of their possessions, including
books. Now, in the last year of his life, Poe was again in dire need.
He had written to John R. Thompson, editor of the *Southern
Literary Messenger*, in January,[19] proposing to continue his
previous "Marginalia" series. Thompson agreed, offering Poe two
dollars per page, and Poe sent copy. On May 10, Poe wrote to
Thompson again, saying, "I forward some more of the
'Marginalia'—rather more piquant, I hope, and altogether more to
my own liking, than what I sent before."[20] Was this judgment a
private joke, since more than one-third of what he was sending was
by "Landor"? Possibly he was also trying to compensate for the
slimness of the manuscript batch, for the installments were dwindl-
ing sadly. The April issue contained six pages (not counting the
reprinted preface), the May issue five and a half, the June issue
four, the July issue three and a half, the August issue nothing, and
the September issue only two pages. In the spring of 1849, then,
Poe apparently had trouble putting those "Marginalia" pages
together. This was not the first time that he had made a commit-
ment which meant money but was unable to produce: his Boston

Lyceum fiasco in the fall of 1845 is well known. Now there were added pressures: illness, unrelieved poverty. "I have met one disappointment after another," he complained to Mrs. Annie Richmond in late April or in May, in the same letter in which he wrote, "I cannot express to you how terribly I have been suffering from gloom. . . . I begin to have a secret terror lest I may *never* behold you again."[21] At the end of June, Poe left for the South, clearly without taking either *Stanley* or the seventh volume of *Burton's* along.

It is likely that Wallace saw or knew of the theft, since Griswold was to note it later in his "Memoir" of Poe.[22] What Wallace's own reaction may have been is a matter for speculation. One would expect that recognizing in the June issue alone seventeen out of thirty-three "Marginalia" items as his own would have produced in him some form of outrage. Such would be the reaction of most writers bent on fame. But we are faced with a man who was working against literary fame, who had let his "William Landor" identity die; and it is equally possible that he received some form of morbid satisfaction from Poe's stealing from him. Or he might have considered the theft a tribute. Seeing the words of his own youth not dead but here born again might even have pleased him. But one cannot help thinking—in terms of his coming suicide—with what inadmissible bitterness! For here was another testimony that "William Landor" was too good a writer to have died, as Horace Binney Wallace was too good a writer to be unknown. What desperate comfort was, in that case, open to him but his secret affinity to Poe?

Possibly, a similar awareness on Poe's part—that the defunct "Landor" had become part of him somehow—had moved Poe in the first place to make so free with "Landor's" words. In late July or August, in Richmond, after he had been unable to supply Thompson with copy for the August issue of the *Southern Literary Messenger* and was squeezing out those two pages for the September issue that would bring him only four dollars instead of ten, why did Poe not plagiarize from another source? He had declared earlier that plagiarism did not necessarily imply "moral delinquency." Stronger than his "moral" openness seems to have been his ontological openness—a sensitivity, like Wallace's, to the reverberations of the Tamerlane-Tyler-Usher-Wilson-Dupin chain, and a readiness to look upon the writings of the long silent "Landor" as his own. Among all the influences and sources that have been studied, there is no other writer from whom Poe appropriated

passages with such persistence. There is almost a kind of klep-
tomania here, whose secret object is closeness. What did Poe
know about "Landor" beyond what he was able to gather from his
writings? Had he and Wallace ever met in person?

Graham's Magazine had its editorial offices in Philadelphia only
three blocks from Walnut and Front Streets, where Wallace and his
brother had their law office, and there were people Wallace and
Poe knew in common—Griswold, above all, but also George P.
Morris, John P. Kennedy, Charles Fenno Hoffman, and many
others; and in New York Poe was frequently a guest at the salon of
Anne Lynch Botta on Waverly Place, together with some of
Wallace's closest friends, Griswold and Morris; and Wallace was
frequently in New York. Common sense urges us to conclude that
Poe and Wallace must have met sometime. But there is not one
shred of evidence to support such a meeting.

We know only about Poe and "Landor," the name Poe finally
made known as mysteriously as Wallace might have wanted him to.
He was writing his last published story, in which he portrays Annie
Richmond, one of the women he loved, in the setting of his own
cottage at Fordham. The date of composition appears to be
January, 1849, corresponding to the composition of the April and
May installments of the "Marginalia." He turned to the writings of
"Landor" for help, and the total mental effect on him of this act
may be gathered from the title he gave to the story he was writing:
"Landor's Cottage."[23]

III   *Rufus Wilmot Griswold*

After Poe's death, when Rufus Wilmot Griswold, his literary executor "sinned against Poe"[24] by creating an unfavorable picture of
him, there followed a century of Poe defenders, whose chief
method has been to set up a small wooden image of Griswold and
knock it down in an outburst of moral indignation. The long list includes Baudelaire, such eminent Poe scholars as James Harrison
and Arthur H. Quinn, and most of Poe's many derivative
biographers; and the single key to their position is sentimentality.

In his "Ludwig" obituary and subsequent "Memoir" Griswold
did of course diabolify Poe—partly out of vindictiveness, partly in
order to create a vivid impression—and Poe had his immediate
defenders such as George R. Graham, N. P. Willis, and John Neal.
But these men had known Poe personally and were understandably

swayed by their positive experiences with him. If the passing of decades after a writer's death puts his works in a clearer perspective, it follows that his biography too should receive the benefit of such perspective—independently of the esteem his works may gain or lose.

One corrective measure against the dual portrait of the angelic Poe and his base traducer has been the study of Griswold's life for its own sake. There have been only two such works: Jacob L. Neu's exploratory article in 1925 and Joy Bayless's full-length biography in 1943.[25] T. O. Mabbott's brief review of the latter suggests him to be the only important Poe scholar of his generation who made the effort to understand Griswold apart from Poe.[26] Although we are primarily concerned with Wallace in this study, the friendship between Wallace and Griswold will hopefully shed some added light also on the relationship between Poe and Griswold. But let us first glance at Griswold's career prior to 1845, when to all appearances he and Wallace first met.

Rufus Wilmot Griswold was born in 1815, the twelfth of a Vermont farmer's fourteen children. The father was a hard-working, practical man; the mother was a great reader and a pious woman. Rufus was thought a difficult child—lovable, but also perverse, stubborn, and unsteady. Letters his mother wrote to him later in life—"Rufus, are you a Christian? Are you prepared to meet your God?"[27]—suggest early seeds of a conflict between a puritanical sense of duty and impulsiveness. Rufus inherited his mother's taste for reading, but not her quiet, steady depth. He was apprenticed to a newspaper to learn printing, then sent, at fifteen, to live with his brother, a merchant of Troy, New York, where he attended the Rensselaer School. A prank caused his dismissal, his brother took him into the firm, but they quarreled; so Rufus went to Albany to live with George G. Foster, a twenty-year-old journalist and future author of *New York by Gaslight*. Griswold later referred to the three years he had spent with Foster as an intellectual relationship characterized by much discussion of literature;[28] Joy Bayless's term is "sentimental friendship." But the sorrowful letter she quotes from Foster to the nineteen-year-old Rufus suggests a homosexual attachment, even if one takes into account the exalted terms in which friendship was frequently expressed during this period: "Griswold, my own Griswold . . . I have loved often and deeply. My heart has burned itself almost to a charred cinder by the flames of passion which have glown within it—and yet I have never felt

towards any human being—man or woman—so strong and absorbing affection as I bear you." The letter ends: "Farewell—
farewell—come to me if you love me."[29] Whether physically con-
summated or not, the relationship appears to have awakened
Griswold's mind and senses, and at the same time deepened his
feeling of guilt, both toward his mother for his life of levity and
toward Foster for abandoning him.

The portrait suggested at this time is that of a young man handsome, charming, bright, dandified, restless. His enormous capacity
for hard work and his determination to succeed in the world of
journalism and literature suggest his father's influence, but
perhaps also penance. A strain of self-castigation, of interpreting
his misfortunes as God's punishment, appears through his subsequent experiences. Cultivating the guise of the romantic outcast,
he moved for the following three years from one town to the next
along the Atlantic seaboard, printing, editing, scandal-mongering,
proclaiming the Whig cause. Facile with his pen and an excellent
conversationalist, he made friends and got jobs easily. In 1837, he
formed one of the most advantageous friendships of his career with
Horace Greely, then editor of the *New Yorker*. Greely took the
young man under his wing, helped him get editorial jobs, made
him his own assistant editor, and advised him on his ventures for
years to come.

In the same year that he met Greely, Griswold married Caroline
Searles, daughter of a sea captain. A quiet, devoted girl, she was
captivated by Griswold's worldly charm and flamboyance. Two
daughters were to be born to them. The year of Griswold's
marriage was the year also of his being licensed as a Baptist
preacher. In Griswold literary interests greatly overshadowed
churchly ones; he never took charge of any permanent parish. But
he did preach occasionally, combining his theological concerns
with his ready eloquence; and later in Philadelphia his staunch
support of the Protestant cause against Irish Catholicism was
rewarded by an honorary D.D. degree. Joy Bayless thinks that one
of Griswold's motives in becoming a licenced preacher was to add
to his income; the shaping factor might, with more probability, be
regarded as an attempt to compensate, in terms of his mother's
Christian faith, for what he recognized in himself as a spiritual
hollowness, or at least excess worldliness.

For the young man, whose chief ambition was to become a
literary anthologist, was something of a human anthologist as well.

To hold the many loosely rather than a few deeply, to move lightly from individual to individual, always to show something new on the next page seemed to give him a sense of power and control. His life was full of sudden departures. In 1840, for example, when his wife had just given birth to their second child and Greely had just extended his tenure on the *New Yorker*, Griswold abruptly left both family and job to move to Philadelphia. His ostensible reason was to find a publisher for his projected *Poets and Poetry of America*, but after he had found one he felt the need to move to Boston, then back again to Philadelphia.

But he was not content to see himself so. Every betrayal of his mother's teaching fanned the flames of the hellfire threatening his fundamentalist soul. His moral dilemma had its literary parallel. What aspired to be his most mature criticism in his *Prose Writers of America* resulted, in Bayless's words, only in "aggressiveness" and "dogmatism," qualities which Bayless attributes to Griswold's "lack of self-reliance" (p. 117)—an interpretation, incidentally, for which she might be indebted to Wallace (*LC*, 240). In any event, one wonders whether Griswold possessed enough critical strength in the first place to rely on.

Undoubtedly the most puzzling event in Griswold's life took place in the winter of 1842, something macabre enough to cause Bayless to conclude that "his mind became unbalanced" (p. 66). The background entails Griswold's living apart from his family from the fall of 1840 to the spring of 1842, when he had an attack of what appeared to be consumption. Terrified by thoughts of approaching death, he went to New York to be nursed by his wife for a few weeks, then returned to Philadelphia. In November, he received news of his wife's death in childbirth. His infant son was dead also. Panic-stricken, he rushed to New York and after the funeral would not leave the cemetery until his wife's uncle commanded him sternly to "have done with this nonsense and come along home." The next night he "found comfort," says Bayless, in expressing his sorrow in writing a poem and also several letters. In these he dwelled guiltily on all that Caroline had done for him while she lived. Griswold returned to Philadelphia mournfully. Forty days after the funeral, a few days before Christmas, he went to New York again, gained entrance to the crypt, and, apparently left alone there, removed the lid of the coffin. Shocked by the state of decomposition of his wife's face, he nevertheless kissed her forehead and "cut off locks of her beautiful hair, damp with death dews."[30] In the process he lost consciousness and was found at the end of the day, his face against his wife's.

The loss of consciousness may have been the result of an epileptic fit, such as Griswold subsequently reported on another occasion.[31] More puzzling is the morbid undertaking itself, the suspension of what he no doubt knew perfectly well about the nature of decomposition. But Bayless's attributing this necrophilic episode to an unbalanced mind is a touch too facile. Since there is no sign of an even remotely similar experience in Griswold's records, the explanation might be more profitably sought in his relationship with Caroline. That he was unable to love her to the extent that he demanded of himself is suggested by his lengthy and apparently compulsive absences from her, for which he undoubtedly felt guilty. Every tear, every written protestation of his love would then only point up his emotional failing—something confirmed by the passing of the chilling weeks after the funeral. Some such threat of an all-pervasive coldness may well have moved him to his desperate, quixotic attempt against the progress of time.

Griswold made two more efforts at married life. He met Charlotte Myers of Georgia probably in 1844 or 1845. She was well-to-do, but twelve years his senior and Jewish, which disturbed Griswold more than he admitted to himself at the time. He made a tentative proposal, then tried to break the engagement. But Charlotte's two aunts insisted on the wedding, which took place in August, 1845. As Bayless puts it, Charlotte "was through some physical misfortune, incapable of being a wife."[32] Since Bayless goes on to say that Charlotte's "incapacity" may not have been known to her or to her aunts beforehand, the malformation, if any, must have been minor, possibly correctable by surgery. At any rate, Griswold eagerly seized upon his "discovery" to obtain a divorce. Charlotte's humiliation, her clinging to Griswold through his younger daughter, finally her revengeful attempt to nullify their divorce after Griswold had remarried make Charlotte appear the more passionate, hence in some ways the more sympathetic, party. Unfortunately for Griswold, when Charlotte's attempt to have their divorce vacated came to trial in 1856, the judge found no record of the divorce, and although he did not doubt that it had been granted, he refused to vacate. This legal ambiguity gave ammunition to Griswold's enemies. After three years of marriage to the wealthy and socially prominent Harriet McCrillis, who had given him a son, he found himself widely accused of living in bigamy.

Instead of fighting the malicious scandal, the prematurely aged, ailing Griswold preferred—characteristically—to separate from Harriet.

Griswold was the type of handsome man whom his friends like to tease about women, an example of which is the invitation Wallace sent him to a ball. But his "amours" notwithstanding, the record of his marriages makes one wonder to what extent he was able to respond to any woman.

Griswold had met Poe in the spring of 1841. The most reliable factual account of the relationship between them remains Killis Campbell's "Poe-Griswold Controversy."[33] However, Campbell makes no attempt to contrast the two men temperamentally, and he makes somewhat artifical divisions between periods of friendly and hostile exchange between them. It is important to bear in mind that Poe with his keener mind and greater depth looked upon Griswold, that charming, shallow upstart, with ambivalence. He could like Griswold well enough to write a favorable review of one of his anthologies—or to borrow money from him; but he could also feel profound irritation and contempt toward him, especially during the period of Griswold's succeeding him as editor of *Graham's Magazine*. And Poe, the vitriolic critic, could be unsparing. Griswold could not afford to reply in kind, for the world would think him a poor critic. Furthermore, his propensity to guilt never failed to make him respond to the downtrodden, and Poe in a sudden childlike reversal of impulse often presented himself as such. As Poe did not hate Griswold, it is hard to believe that Griswold hated Poe. If Griswold had trouble loving, he had trouble hating too.[34] He was nobody's "evil genius."[35] But he was something of a professional gossip, and for all his pains with Poe he took the opportunity to spread those "shocking bad stories"[36] which were not hard to hear or to exaggerate about Poe.

IV *Wallace as Griswold's Ghost*

There was a temperamental difference between Griswold and Wallace also, but instead of clashing, opposites fused in this case into a kind of literary entity. Wallace aspired to no editorial post, he wanted no fame, he was content in many instances, as has been noted, to make Griswold his living mask. Griswold had some difficulty understanding Wallace's secretiveness, but he seemed all the more to admire his genius.[37] Wallace was in turn benevolent,

occasionally stern, sometimes even condescending toward
Griswold.

The first time he felt inclined to write a review for Griswold, he
had an apparently easy task. The book was Griswold's edition of
Milton's prose works,[38] and Wallace felt it acceptable to concen-
trate on juxtaposing Milton's poetic conservatism and his political
liberalism and to dismiss Griswold at the end with a thanks and a
commendation for his "felicity" and his "spirit" (LC, 124). Only
by reading Poe's review of the same work (Works, XII, 245 - 47)
does one realize to what an extent Wallace was evading a number
of Griswold's controversial assertions, such as the invisibility of
Milton's Arianism in his great works, or Milton's being "the
greatest of all human beings" and Bacon's being "the meanest of
mankind."

It is possible that Wallace helped Griswold put together his Prose
Writers of America. He may have advised him on the selection of
authors, even written some of the comments. Griswold's
characteristic ebullience, relatively simple syntax, and ready use of
superlatives such as "wonderful" give way occasionally to a more
meticulous, complex style studded with legal learning. Reading
Wallace's review of the anthology, one forms the impression that
on Chief Justice Marshall and on Hugh S. Legaré, the South
Carolina statesman and critic, Wallace is quoting at great length
not Griswold, as he claims, but himself. Wallace's role in some of
Griswold's other literary projects and the elaborate dedication
Griswold attempted to make to Wallace would support this
possibility.

The book, with its reduced, noncommittal dedication, appeared
early in 1847. During the spring and summer months it received
both praise and blame, as it became an issue in the literary war raging just then in New York, with Poe on one side and Lewis Gaylord
Clark, editor of the Knickerbocker, and Griswold on the other as
chief belligerents.[39] Evert A. Duyckinck wrote an especially severe
review in the Literary World for March 20, and Griswold probably
appealed to Wallace for aid. Wallace waited with characteristic
strategy for the enemy to exhaust itself, then swung into action.
Putting together some of his previously published articles, among
them his 1844 sketch of Willis and his recent comments on Poe,
and adding much new material, he welded them into one mam-
moth review—a kind of magnum opus of reviewing that by its
sheer extent would stamp out all opposition. This is presumably the

version we see in *Literary Criticisms* (pp. 3 - 55). Wallace begins by praising Griswold for having performed a national service and for having executed it ably, "and in many parts brilliantly." But soon his struggle between friendship and literary conscience comes to a head in another kind of evasion: "We acknowledge Mr. Griswold to be a good critic; and if his personal friends or others claim for him the title of a writer of first-rate merit, we make no other hesitation than that we have not yet seen quite enough of original matter from his pen" (*LC*, 4).

The Prose Writers of America, observed Perry Miller shrewdly, "is a sly, a casuistical and brazen demonstration that the tradition of American prose is at bottom conservative, is Whiggish."[40] Wallace's review of it, we might add, is even more brazenly "Whiggish"—pleased that the new American literature "will bear no resemblance to the productions of 'Young America,' a fraternity young only in wisdom, and incapable of representing anything of America but its vulgarity" (*LC*, 6). In addition, the review is shapeless, subjective, and at times irrelevant. The incorporation of the Willis article, for example, gives Willis over seven pages out of the total fifty, whereas Hawthorne—admittedly, the author only of stories at this time—is dismissed in a sentence. James D. Nourse, a young protégé of Wallace, is given a page, although he is not represented in the anthology. Washington Allston, the painter, who is represented on the strength of his novel, *Monaldi*, launches Wallace on a discussion of American art for another seven pages. Daniel Webster, one of Wallace's heroes—recently defeated in the Girard inheritance case before the U.S. Supreme Court by none other than Horace Binney—receives a similarly large portion.

And yet, at a time of puffery and casuistry, when reviews consisted of mere lengthy quotations and authors frequently planted anonymous reviews of their own works, Wallace's approach was not unusual. For the present-day reader, the critical value comes through in spots, when Wallace is not being political or partisan. Against his own dislike of Transcendentalism, specifically youthful impatience with Channing, he is able here to view Channing as a great philosophical innovator. With his apparently unassuming method of reducing "affection and intellect to one," Channing, says Wallace, originated a new analysis that has such far-reaching consequences in philosophical, social, and political problems as to have introduced "a new element into our civlization" (*LC*, 19 - 20). Coming to writers of fiction, Wallace is especially perceptive

about the works of Charles Brockden Brown and Cooper, seeing in
one a "great ingenuity of mental contrivance" at the expense of
"the invigoration of human sympathy"; in the other, "a
copiousness and energy of imagination." Cooper is admired greatly
for the difficult task of writing about "regions bare of association"
and of breathing into "the vulgar or repulsive or disgusting" the
"roseate air of romance" (LC, 21 - 22). But the overall value of the
review lies in its major theme—which underneath his personal
preferences and political partisanship Wallace sounded again and
again in his reviews—that there was in America a new, dynamic,
individual literature being created, which could no longer be
thought of as a mere offshoot of English literature but was in-
digenously American.

In its original version the review was apparently thought too
long, and Wallace deleted half, including the already published
portions and some others dealing mainly with art. As it was then
printed in the Knickerbocker Magazine, in five installments
through 1847 and 1848,[41] the review is far more balanced, although
Webster is still given a whole installment, whereas Poe is reduced
to a mere mention. Willis receives a still worse fate. Instead of
seven pages of essential praise, he receives in the Knickerbocker
version a passage that refers to "the beauty-spots of his writings" as
"pimples of an over-fed fancy" and compares him to "a footman
who has dressed himself in his master's satin waistcoat, and is playing off the airs which he learned behind a chair" (31, 350). It is difficult to account for Wallace's sharp reversal of attitude within a
month or two. One may speculate about a possible quarrel between
Willis and Wallace's friend Morris; or between Willis and
Griswold, in light of their future conflict after Poe's death.

When the review was reprinted in the Southern Literary
Messenger in 1850,[42] it was further abridged, with the Webster
passage scrupulously updated. To Webster's previous merits, including his support of a high tariff and his attempts as Secretary of
State to maintain a Whig position in President Tyler's democratic
administration, there was now added praise for his recent defense
in the Senate of the Constitutional rights of the South—ironically,
just what had caused many to call him a traitor to the North.

The highly confidential literary relationship between Wallace
and Griswold intensified during 1847 - 49. Shortly after his arrival
in New York in the summer of 1847, Griswold solicited Wallace's
opinion about establishing a quarterly. On August 11, Wallace

replied more than enthusiastically, offering to write an article for each number, or perhaps as many as three or four. It is as though the idea of a quarterly had stirred some deep need to power in him, as he gives specific directions to Griswold about the length of articles, what should be paid per page, what contributors to solicit—in an almost "manic" tone:

Grace Greenwood, decidedly—something on feminine authors, or feminine natures, manners or what not—Tell her not to make a solemn, grave, sensible article, but one lively, dashing, fantastic, crammed with puns, quips, & quirks—only good,—careful & striking. Such articles must be in, for variety.—Suppose you try old Webster. Write him a confidential letter—frank & sincere. Tell him the object is to start a really conservative journal—to guide & lead.[43]

A year later Wallace saw himself more in an editorial capacity, with the nature of his need for power emerging more distinctly: "I am heartily desirous to set, or see set, in operation of a strong, permanent journal. I wish it as a means of acting powerfully upon the opinions & conduct of the nation."[44] He was against putting out a mere trial number or two, and possibly because of a lack of capital the project never materialized.

More fruitful was the project on Washington, which Griswold undertook for the publishers Carey and Hart in competition with a work by the historian Joel T. Headley, *Washington and his Generals*.[45] Under Griswold's editorship, the anonymous rival work appeared at the end of 1847, in two volumes, entitled *Washington and the Generals of the American Revolution*. It was successful enough to see ten editions to 1885. Wallace is the author of the sixty-page leading essay on Washington;[46] the sketches on seventy-seven generals are by various writers including Griswold himself and, most interestingly, William Gilmore Simms.[47]

Wallace's essay, an essentially factual account of Washington's military achievements, is a reminder of Wallace's preoccupation with bold, decisive, physical action within the confines of his own withdrawn, contemplative life. He sees Washington as a practical man, "in no degree speculative," and venerates him all the more. Equally interesting is the aristocratic Wallace's sudden swing into faith in collective judgment—an example of which appears in his essay on plagiarism, where the public is endowed with a power to detect an imposture as well as a false alarm. Here he asserts that

when a "true hero appears among mankind," he is first recognized
not by individual intellect, but by "the general sense of humanity"
(*ASE*, 443).

Wallace's interest in warfare comes through even more clearly in
the book he wrote in its entirety for Griswold, *Napoleon and the
Marshals of the Empire*. Some of the correspondence about this
book gives a good insight into Wallace's ghostwriting for Griswold.
Carey and Hart, wishing to compete with Headley's earlier
Napoleon and his Marshals as well, approached Griswold on the
subject in the fall of 1847. Griswold turned to Wallace. Apparently
the publishers wanted to meet the author, for on October 15
Griswold wrote to Abraham Hart: "I am sorry that my friend
'Junius' declines to have more than a single confidant; so the
Marshals must be Marshaled by another."[48] The publishers apparently withdrew their request and Wallace set to work. When we
consider that all communications between the two parties, who
were both in Philadelphia, had to be channeled through Griswold,
who was in New York, the arrangement assumes a comical dimension. On November 24, Carey and Hart inquired how "the
gentleman who is writing Napoleon & his Marshalls for us" was
progressing,[49] and on December 19 Griswold assured them that
"the book, though prepared rapidly, will give you perfect satisfaction," adding, "The author desires me to inquire when he may
draw (through me) for the payment."[50] According to the
publishers, the author was to be paid upon returning the corrected
proofs. On January 4, 1848, Griswold wrote to them: "I am very
sorry that my friend 'Junius' does not prove so tractable as I hoped.
He stipulated in the beginning that I should arrange for his being
paid on the completion of his labors, and he has worked night and
day to receive for the beginning of the year his 500 $." Griswold
assumed responsibility for this misunderstanding and asked Carey
and Hart either to accept the author's stipulation or to give him a
written note to the effect of their interpretation of the agreement,
offering in either case to pay the interest on the sum involved.[51]
The matter was resolved somehow and the book appeared on April
15, 1848, in two volumes.

If the repressed man in Wallace, with conveniently classical
ideals, may be held responsible for the disparagement and the flip-
pancy about Napoleon in his earlier writings, the romantic in him
now came fully to the fore. The more clearly one understands
Wallace, the more natural it seems that he should have wanted to

make Napoleon a subject for serious study. Napoleon, who fascinated a whole century, who still fascinates, was a specific answer to everything bold, decisive, and free smoldering in Wallace's own secret depths. Already, thirty-odd years after Waterloo, Wallace saw a need for historical perspective, for the age had become "commercial and industrial," and the thesis that "war is the true profession of a gentleman" had become relegated to "the romantic that lingers in our fancies" (I, 12). Early in the work, Wallace makes a careful distinction: "Nothing is more simple than the *science* of war; nothing is more complicated than the *art* of war." A confusion between the two has resulted in both in "irrational and extravagant wonder" at Napoleon and in underestimation among some English writers of his genius (I, 54 - 55). Between these two extremes Wallace himself maintains a balanced position as he traces Napoleon's military, then political career through the nearly three hundred-page leading essay. This first portion of the book is somewhat disjointed, for the major campaigns after those of Italy and Egypt are systematically postponed to later chapters dealing with Napoleon's twenty-six marshals; but this device has the advantage of unifying the work. Although not as popular in appeal as Headly's rival work on the same subject, the book went through several editions to 1885. "It is a keen, accurate, well-written production," wrote the reviewer for *Graham's Magazine.* "It is evidently the work of a person who understands military operations. . . . Its defect consists in the leniency of its judgment on that gigantic public criminal. Napoleon was a grand example of a great man, who demonstrated, on a wide theatre of action, what can be done in this world by a colossal intellect and an iron will without any moral sense."[52] It is almost as if the reviewer had been thinking of Tyler, as another one of Wallace's self-projections. And perhaps he had. In any event, although the work says little about Napoleon's or his marshals' personal lives, it contains vivid descriptions and dramatic scenes reminiscent of Wallace's best fiction. We get a detail, for example, of the fall of Toulon in 1793, which won Napoleon his promotion to brigadier general:

It was determined by the English to destroy all the magazines and shipping which were likely to fall into the hands of the French. In the evening the arsenal was blown up, and nine seventy-four-gun ships and four frigates of the French squadron were fired. The explosions from the arsenals resembled the successive eruptions of a volcano, and the magnificent vessels blazing for several hours in the roads, lighted up the scene with terrible splendor. Meanwhile, the incessant discharge of cannon from l'Eguillette and Balagnier upon the harbor, and from Fort Malbosquet, which had been abandoned by the allies, upon the town, completed the horror of that memorable night. At break of day the English fleet, bearing away a great number of inhabitants, was seen out at sea; and the city of Toulon was in the hands of the Convention. (I, 38 - 39)

We get an unforgettable glimpse of Napoleon in Egypt in 1808:

One day, while seated in the divan of the grand-sheiks, he was told that the Arabs of the tribe of Osnadis had killed a fellah and carried off some flocks: with an air of indignation, he instantly ordered a staff-officer to march with three hundred horsemen and two hundred dromedaries into the Bahireh, to punish the guilty parties, and obtain reparation. The sheik Elmodi said to him, with a laugh, "Was this fellah thy cousin, that his death excites so much anger in thee?"—"He was more," replied Napoleon; "all whom I command are my children."—"Good!" said the sheik, "that is spoken like the prophet himself." (I, 141-42)

We see the defeated Emperor on the retreat from Moscow in 1812:

Ney remained behind. It was impossible to wait for him, and with infinite regret the emperor ordered the army to continue its advance to Liady and Orcha. Napoleon marched on foot, with a stick in his hand, walking with difficulty, and halting every quarter of an hour, as if unwilling to leave his old companion-in-arms to his fate; every moment the name of Ney escaped from his lips with exclamations of grief. (II, 204)

Wallace's authorship of works that appeared under Griswold's name seems to have increased Wallace's sense of power over his friend. It was now he who suggested to Griswold another, presumably ghostwritten history of the recently concluded Mexican War[53]—a work which, however, never materialized. His letters to Griswold—typically, none from Griswold to him has survived—remain kindly, but more and more commanding in tone. He readily calls Griswold's *Female Poets of America* "admirable and beautiful," enclosing a review of it for Griswold to insert in the *Tribune* and promising another,[54] and he is pleased to supply items for Griswold's projected biographical dictionary;[55] but he expects services in return, sometimes asking for a whole series of them in one letter. In supporting the publisher and economist Henry Carey in his stand against the Camden and Amboy Railway monopoly, for example, Wallace solicits Griswold's aid with perfect self-confidence: "I should be extremely glad to have access to any respectable New York paper, to give him what aid is in my power."[56] Of a review written by James D. Nourse, which he has promised to place, he writes in the same letter: "My principal reliance will be on you," and gives instructions as to how it should be inserted and where it should be sent.

And yet the intimacy, even affection, betrayed by Wallace's commanding tones is carefully concealed from others. In his letter to Richard Henry Dana, Jr. about the elder Dana's lecture series on Shakespeare, which he was organizing in Philadelphia in the fall of 1849, Wallace is condescending toward his friend, almost ashamed of knowing him too well:

Mr. Griswold some time ago, when in Philadelphia, expressed to me his very strong desire to be allowed to testify his interest in the occasion by sending any services which he might be allowed. We, of course, all are very well acquainted with Mr. Griswold, & would probably take quite the same view. There is much that is interesting about him. His eager, enthusiast loyalty to all that he recognizes as superior in ability & accomplishment, engages sympathy; & knowing his profound & ardent appreciation of Mr. Dana's genius, I did not hesitate to say to him that the design would be happy to have the honour of his countenance. I have no doubt that he will in all respects be willing to be guided by suggestions from ourselves.[57]

Quite different in tone is Wallace's letter to Griswold, written presumably after the Danas had agreed to his services:

I enclose a copy of the Dana Correspondence, which appears in all our papers this morning. I hope you will puff & blast away in all manner of styles. Insert something in the Tribune's Correspondence, & in the Tribune editorially.

Can you get Jarvis to write on the subject for the Ledger?

Get something in the Literary World. . . . [58]

V   *The Poe "Betrayal"*

Poe died in Baltimore, on October 7, 1849; two days later there appeared in the *New York Tribune* Griswold's notorious obituary

signed "Ludwig." In fairness to Griswold, we must note that when
he received news of Poe's death he was in the midst of a controversy of international proportions. The affair involved the strained
personal relations between Secretary of State John M. Clayton and
the French minister to the United States, William Tell Poussin.
Aggravated by the illegal sale of some tobacco by American agents
in Mexico, the controversy came to a head when Clayton accused
Poussin of insulting the U.S. Government and procured his dismissal. Although public opinion favored Secretary Clayton, Poussin
had his defenders, among them Griswold. Possibly on the very day
that he wrote the Poe obituary, he wrote also a defense of Poussin
for the *New York Evening Post,* which was printed in four columns
on October 9, the same day that the Poe obituary appeared in the
Tribune, and was also signed "Ludwig." This detail would support
the "haste" that Griswold later claimed about his composition of
the Poe obituary; but we must carry Griswold's involvement in the
Clayton-Poussin affair a few steps further in order to see that in
some ways it both foreshadows and parallels his famous Poe controversy. Griswold's defense of Poussin was answered on October
18 by one of the *Tribune's* regular correspondents, who signed
himself "Alpha," charging that "Ludwig" had been hired by
Poussin and that Clayton knew of this.

Griswold had thus stumbled into a difficulty that Wallace did
not believe he could handle by himself. Wallace wrote to him the
next day: "I did not, until last night, see the Tribune correspondent 'Alpha' in the paper of yesterday. I wish you would take the
enclosed, as it stands, in my handwriting, to the Tribune & require
its insertion." Wallace was looking out for both Poussin and
Griswold, for he added: "It is due to M. Poussin," and also: "I
hope you will not make any publication on the subject *under your
own name.* What a miserable scrape Willis had got into from coming out under his own name, against an anonyme. You had better
not publish anything; I will try to take care of all parties."[59]

What appeared in the *Tribune* on October 22 was an editorial
frame, within which "Ludwig" denied the charge, warning that "if
the Secretary of State has declared or intimated that the writer of
those remarks was hired, paid, or in any manner employed by Mr.
Poussin, the Secretary of State is doubly a slanderer." The "editor"
went on to observe that these remarks showed "the hand of a
lawyer, and we have been informed that 'to oppose them one must
grapple with one of the first legal minds of this country.'"

"Alpha" was silenced, but what is more interesting is Wallace's strategic reliance on masks—not just a single one this time but a whole series of them—and his readiness, once securely disguised, to claim his own legal eminence.

The Poe obituary, which had appeared in the same paper not quite two weeks previously, begins by stating that "few will be grieved" by Poe's death because "he had few or no friends," and his death will be regretted primarily because "in him literary art lost one of its most brilliant but erratic stars." The rest of the two-column obituary develops this statement. After a sketch of Poe's life, as accurate as the romanticised data Poe himself had sent Griswold eight years previously, Griswold shows Poe as a conversationalist of "supra-mortal" eloquence, then as a "dreamer dwelling . . . in heaven or hell," who "walked the streets in madness or melancholy," muttering curses or prayers for those he idolized, or "all night, with drenched garments and arms wildly beating the winds and rains," communed with spirits of "Aidenn." Fitting a passage from "The Raven" into his portraiture, Griswold then speaks of Poe's mind as bereft "of all faith in man or woman," and compares Poe in a quoted passage to Vivian in Bulwer's *Caxtons.* Finally, he reaffirms Poe's great achievement in fiction, reduces him as a critic to "a carping grammarian," but pays him high tribute as a poet (*Works*, I, 348-59).

Perhaps the most telling and succinct recent comment on the "Ludwig" obituary is T. O. Mabbott's exclamation that an obituary should be written in such manner.[60] Rightfully, Mabbott places emphasis not on Griswold's unjustified or justified vindictiveness, but on decorum. Clearly the greatest offense in decorum is the Bulwer passage depicting Vivian as beautiful, daring, with a "fiery atmosphere" about him, but envious, arrogant, irascible, cynical, sneering, dishonorable, and ambitious so that he might "despise a world which galled his self-conceit"(*Works*, I, 357). Indecorum assumes a dimension of the ridiculous when one realizes that elsewhere in his novel Bulwer speaks of Vivian as one who lacks imagination and as one who has no interest in literature.[61] Whether Griswold was aware of Vivian's total characterization or not, this quick reaching for the poignant clearly shows him to be the hasty, superficial writer that he was. The rest of the portraiture is similarly synthetic, stringing together fragments of Poe's own highly charged diction but without Poe's controlling art.

And yet with characteristic journalistic facility and sense of timing Griswold had seized on one of the great fascinations of the age still alien to these shores: the diabolic genius. Within two days of his death Poe was made into a dark legend.

Replies to "Ludwig," whose identity was generally known, began to mount in defense of Poe. Among them there was an especially poignant one by Willis in the *Home Journal* on October 20, and Wallace came to his friend's aid. His method was characteristic—a supposedly objective portrait, with only two casual references to the controversy over Poe. Wallace sent the article to George Rex Graham's brother William, who was apparently about to publish a "Gallery" of some sort, on October 29, sending a copy to Griswold on the same day. In the accompanying letter Wallace refers to the article jokingly as "a vile libel on your character," adding, "I am conscious of having done no justice to you: but I determined at the beginning not to make a panegyric, & I believe I have kept my word."[62] Since William Graham's "Gallery" never saw light, the article found its way to the *Knickerbocker Magazine*, where it appeared almost a year later, in August, 1850.[63]

According to his intention, Wallace admits certain frailties in Griswold, chiefly his superficiality: "His perceptions are keenly intelligent, and full of vitality and vividness; but they are too mercurial, fugitive, and hasty" (*LC*, 239). Rather than attributing these shortcomings to corresponding ones of temperament, Wallace explains that Griswold is not yet fulfilled as a writer, that he suffers from a "want of mental self-reliance," and that he is one of those otherwise superior people whose actions tend to misfire because "some unlucky element mixes itself up with the operation, some trick of weakness displays itself, some false bias, some fatal affinity comes athwart the effort . . . and the movement which commenced from genius concludes in commonplace" (*LC*, 240-41).

Praise for Griswold predominates of course. He has helped the cause of American literature through his anthologies; he has done much to help other writers; he is free of partiality, prejudice, and literary jealousy; and he is a loyal friend. Referring to Griswold's recent appointment as Poe's literary executor, Wallace writes:

If the time and talents of a skillful editor, who will labor *gratuitously*, in some benevolent undertaking toward the works of some defunct, are needed, Dr. Griswold is counted upon with ready confidence. The case of the late Edgar Allen [sic] Poe is an illustration of this matter, very honorable to the subject of our notice. There was nothing in the private relations of the parties to render it at all natural or probable that Mr. Poe should have left a request that Dr. Griswold would be the editor of his writings: but he knew the generous spirit and admirable capacity of the person whose regard he invoked, and felt assured that he would do in the best manner what probably no other would do at all. (*LC*, 233 - 34)

Later Wallace refers to the "Ludwig" obituary: "What a profound, complete and exquisite estimate of the character of Poe" (*LC*, 242).

Composed in the month of Poe's death, these relatively controlled passages—followed by a reference to Poe's defenders as "the *canaille* of scribblers"—reveal such bitter feeling toward Poe that we are led to suspect that Wallace had previously expressed them to Griswold and that they perhaps form a shaping element in the "Ludwig" obituary itself. Yet these passages remain the only evidence, and if one would probe Wallace's psyche at the time of Poe's death he can but resume the speculation over Wallace's discovery of Poe's unabashed plagiarisms from him. That Poe had brought Wallace's "Landor" self back to him is very likely. The circumstances of his relationship to Poe were before him, forming a bizarre chain of affinity, theft, triumph, and death. The only question is how much Wallace felt them through, whether he saw them in the light of his own approaching doom. Was Poe to him the hated rival who had soared in his stead and now lay fallen at his feet? Wallace's victory would last for a short time only—until his own far more terrible end would make Poe once again triumph in literary immortality.

Within three months of Poe's death, the first two volumes of the Griswold edition, containing most of the tales and poems, came off the press of J. S. Redfield. By way of prefatory matter, Griswold reprinted an earlier article about Poe by James Russell Lowell and Willis's defense of October 20 with its quoted passages from the "Ludwig" obituary. Griswold's motive was no doubt to demonstrate his own fairness in the controversy, but his scheme misfired, for Willis's words provided all the greater incentive for further attacks on "Ludwig." Griswold turned to Wallace for help.

Wallace's advice receives illumination from another controversy in which Griswold had found himself recently. Sometime in January, 1850, Griswold committed the impropriety of comparing Jefferson to the "atheist" Thomas Paine, for which he was taken to task by several papers. On February 5 he replied to these in the *New York Tribune*, stating that Jefferson was not a Christian and that there existed proof that Jefferson had secretly collaborated with Philip Freneau in the latter's *National Gazette* in a series of abusive attacks on Washington. There were replies to this, and Griswold appealed to Wallace, who advised,

Wait until the enemy has printed all that he intends to print. *Then*—do not make a new article in the shape of a mere answer to the Ledger's articles; but revise & extend your original article taking notice of any new matter introduced by the Ledger, & replying to it in connexion with the matter in your original paper. You will thus avoid the directly controversial form. . . . You will in this manner make a paper of permanent & historical value. . . . Take your time: prepare your answer deliberately: & fill the gun full.[64]

Waiting for the enemy to exhaust himself and then stepping forth in the guise of objectivity is precisely the strategy Wallace offered in the Poe controversy also. That Griswold's appeal was desperate is suggested by Wallace's "My dear friend" in his reply of May 4—the only such salutation in any of his extant letters to Griswold. He wrote,

In regard to these fellows who are discussing your article on Poe, I think the way to deal with them is this. To let a third person review the whole subject.—Yr. article, Willis's, Graham's, & Neal's—in a distant & impartial way—setting the thing in the true light. I would do it with great pleasure. But I should require to be furnished with *all* the 4 articles in question. I leave here on Monday evening next, & sail on Wednesday following. . . . I could write an article while I am at sea, & send it over by the first steamer.[65]

Wallace had mentioned in a previous letter that he was about to sail to Europe, suggesting that Griswold accompany him. "It would do your health much good."[66] But Griswold remained in New York. Whether he accepted Wallace's offer of a "distant and impartial" review of the controversy is doubtful, for such an article is not to be found. Griswold seems, however, to have taken to heart some of Wallace's suggestions about donning the mask of objectivity as he set about to write his seventy-page "Memoir" of Poe for the forthcoming third volume of the edition.

It was in this "Memoir" that Griswold committed the further indiscretion of altering some of the letters Poe had written to him, which damned him forever in the eyes of such modern investigators as Campbell and Quinn and their followers. Griswold probably strayed into his textual tampering by degrees, with

Wallace's fondness for masks and editorial frames a possible factor. Wallace probably did not know about his friend's forgeries, and would have disapproved had he known, but one wonders if his handling of the Poussin controversy, for example, did not embolden Griswold in permitting himself "editorial" manipulations with regard to Poe. They were probably innocent at first—the changing of a date for greater clarity or emphasis—the justifiable deletion of an inconvenient passage—the addition of a few innocent words to put himself in a more important light, and, incidentally, Poe in a kindlier one; then perhaps arose such temptations as inventing a whole letter, or paying off an old score to Evert Duyckinck of the *Literary World* by making Poe speak ill of him, or making Poe speak ill of George R. Graham and Louis Godey as well, so as to ward off further attacks. "Fill the gun full," Wallace had advised during the Jefferson controversy. With what delight this sorcerer's apprentice must have divided and conquered while his master was abroad.

Yet in fairness to Griswold it must be noted that in terms of nineteenth-century requirements, which were far less exacting than those of today, he performed the purely editorial part of his task well. Killis Campbell admits as much; and the editors of Poe's *Collected Works*, T. O. Mabbott and his successor, Burton R. Pollin, have given preference to Griswold's text, rather than to Harrison's, in many instances.

The third volume of Poe's works was coming out in September, 1850, and Griswold, in possession of Wallace's sketch of him originally intended for William Graham, arranged for its publication in the August issue of the *Knickerbocker* and again in the September 28 issue of the *Home Journal* to provide himself with dual cover. What particularly concerns us here is the absence from the third volume of about half of the "Marginalia" items that Poe had taken from Wallace. In the "Memoir" Griswold makes a direct reference to these, saying: "I have omitted in the republication of these papers, numerous paragraphs which were rather compiled than borrowed from one of the profoundest and wisest of our own scholars."[67]

This sentence provides the last link on record between Griswold and Wallace. Ten days after Wallace's death Griswold married his third wife, and the article he had promised to write about Wallace did not get written. In the winter or early spring of 1853, Herman Hooker wrote to Griswold, saying: "I have been disappointed in not seeing your notice of Wallace."[68] On April 29, Hooker wrote to

Griswold again: "I thought it a somewhat unaccountable thing that you who never let the works or name of a friend slip and perish for want of a record—should not have been heard on that noble & just theme—Wallace and his genius."[69]

One wonders if Griswold, whose morbid tendencies underneath his flitting had once led him to open his wife's tomb, found himself unable to cope with Wallace's particularly frightful manner of death. That at the same time he felt liberated by Wallace's death is also possible. Wallace's influence had been heavy, restrictive, paternal. Griswold was of course busy with other matters—his brilliant new marriage, his opportunity to ride with Poe to further glory. In the year of Hooker's letters he brought out a new edition of the first three volumes of Poe's works, then set about assembling a fourth volume, which was to appear 1856, completing the edition.

Ironically, Griswold was not permitted to flit long. The judgment sounded by his mother's words, "Rufus, are you a Christian?" which he had alternately clutched and run from, caught up with him in the form of illness and premature old age. Before his death in 1857, at the age of forty-two, he appointed George H. Moore and Wallace's surviving brother John to be his literary executors. In a letter to the elder Dana, John Wallace expressed surprise over the appointment, saying that he knew little about Griswold's literary work.[70] But Griswold had known the closeness that had existed between the brothers, and his gesture—characteristic in its pathos—seems to have been his last, confused appeal to Wallace both living and dead.

CHAPTER 4

The Lawyer as Journalist and Critic

I Law Books

ABOUT the time of the demise of "William Landor,"
Wallace turned to the production of law books. Besides the
example of his brother's legal scholarship, a factor may have been
Wallace's disillusionment with "the hapless trade" of magazine
writing. Still, when we consider the nearly fifty volumes that Wallace edited or re-edited in collaboration during the eight remaining
years of his life, we cannot help seeing them as an avenue to a
passionate, creative spirit's doom. But if it was the devil's doing,
the temptation included much: money of course, but more importantly, safety in an intellectual corner from the agony of imaginative writing, which might not even be acknowledged.

Wallace's editorship of law books is always coupled with the
name of J. I. Clark Hare. Son of the distinguished chemist, Robert
Hare, John Innes Clark Hare was in Wallace's class at the University of Pennsylvania, from which he graduated in 1834. Like
Wallace, Hare studied chemistry first, then law. We get a glimpse
of the two friends in the fall of 1836 on a visit to Wallace's cousin
Mary, daughter of the Boston antiquary, Lucius Manlius Sargent.
"Books and work were joyfully thrown aside, and . . . nothing was
thought of but talking with all our might, and rambling over hill
and dale," wrote Mary Sargent from Roxbury to her aunt,
Wallace's mother.[1] The one sad note to this idyllic morning is
Mary's death of consumption five years later.[2] Hare and Wallace
became related in 1842, when Hare married Esther Coxe Binney,
Horace Binney's daughter. Collaboration between Hare and
Wallace seems to have grown out of a close friendship and common
legal attitudes. After Wallace's death Hare continued the work,
sometimes in collaboration with John Wallace. Subsequently Hare
became presiding judge of the district court of Philadelphia,

professor of law at the University of Pennsylvania, then provost of
the Philadelphia Law Academy. After his death in 1905, he was
pronounced one of the greatest judges Philadelphia had produced.[3]

Referring to the first part of the nineteenth century as the "formative era" of American law, Roscoe Pound enumerates six contributions made by doctrinal writing in general: the swaying of all
American jurisdictions except that of Louisiana toward the adop-
tion of common law; the providing of courts with "authoritative
statements of received common law"; the preventing of
"premature crude codification"; the preservation of unity in
American law; the saving of equity from Puritan prejudice against
"personal standard"; and the saving of American private law from
inexperienced legislative experimentation.[4]

Wallace and Hare saw the need to extend and develop the
pioneering work of such jurists as James Kent and Joseph Story;
consequently they set about to make a great body of English cases
available for American use. They began with John W. Smith's
Selection of Leading Cases in Various Branches of the Law, a recent work,[5] which was to become an English legal classic, with a
thirteenth edition published as late as 1939. In republishing this
work in two volumes in 1844, Wallace and Hare added notes of
their own and made references to American decisions. They turned
next to an extensive series under the general title, *Reports of Cases
Argued and Determined in the Courts of Exchequer and Exchequer Chamber*, again relating them to decisions in American
courts and sometimes providing tables of cases. Wallace and Hare
brought out the first set, covering the years 1836 to 1847, in sixteen
volumes, during 1845-49.[6] Five additional sets followed, covering
current as well as previous years, the total number of volumes
amounting during Wallace's life to thirty-one. Conjointly with the
Exchequer reports, Wallace and Hare brought out in 1847 their
most important two volumes, *American Leading Cases . . . in
Several Departments of the Law; with Especial Reference to Mer-
cantile Law*. Finally, they undertook another, more specialized,
edition of English cases, Frederick T. White and Owen D. Tudor's
Selection of Leading Cases in Equity.[7] The work with additional
notes and references to American decisions appeared in three
volumes, during 1849-51. These four projects all went through
future editions, some of them during Wallace's lifetime, the majori-
ty of them after his death, carrying his and Hare's names into the
1870's and 1880's.

Since Wallace and Hare usually edited specific volumes individually, these were reviewed individually also. It is therefore possible to read what might be more impartial commentary on Wallace's legal writing than Horace Binney's high praise for it in his "Obituary." For example, the *American Law Journal*, noting the first volume of the American appearance of Tudor's *Leading Cases in Equity*, speaks of Wallace's "dilligence, care and discrimination which are the unerring marks of a well trained legal mind which comprehends something more than mere cases . . . which apprehends clearly and enunciates carefully and accurately a principle . . . which is of practical and substantial value in the everyday concerns of human life."[8]

If such "very tedious" work had an adverse effect on Wallace's inner self, this effect was aggravated by the very fruits of the achievement. With his name already on the title pages of impressive professional tomes, Wallace wrote in a review of Samuel Warren's *A Popular and Practical Introduction to Law Studies*, "There are many ways of making legal martinets and *petit-maitres*, but there is only one way to make a lawyer, and that is, earnest, concentrated, continued hard labor."[9] Throughout the review, Wallace emphasizes the idea of hard labor, harsh discipline, and subjugation of self more and more fervently, as though trying to derive comfort from punishing others as he was punishing himself.

II   *The* Home Journal

If "Monologues among the Mountains" was a desperate cry in the night, Wallace's journalism was a more practicable compromise between his legal labors and his need to write. The opportunity was Morris's new publishing venture, the *National Press*—later, with Willis's co-editorship, renamed the *Home Journal*[10]—to which Wallace contributed, between the years 1846 and 1851, no less than sixty-five and probably closer to one hundred anonymous editorials and reviews. The editorials are Wallace's most public writing, in regard both to subject and to manner. They were partly an act of friendship toward Morris, probably rendered at least initially without pay; partly a patriotic public service; partly a "means," as Wallace wrote in a letter to Griswold, "of acting powerfully upon the opinions & conduct of the nation." Speaking of the press as a "Committee of Public Safety" in America, he avows it his duty as one "who can handle a pen" to direct the course of his countrymen in "advancing their condition to the highest good." Specifically, he aims "to correct the excesses of enthusiasm, to abate the violence of false notions before they overrun into actions, to point out neglected fields of effort and to urge to their occupancy" (*ASE*, 293). The editorials consequently advocate correctives ranging from art education to public parks to railroad comforts to dignity in political elections, always from the point of view of a cultured conservative in face of the somewhat bewildering phenomenon of a brash new society. But if Wallace's tone becomes at times irritatingly paternalistic, his ideals are high, and in the happiest instances of his writing his patriotic concern does transcend his political stance. His criticism of American life is generally constructive, and his defense of America against foreign censure is unfailingly impassioned.

One of his persistent pleas is that the urban population learn to enjoy nature—specifically, that they escape during the summer months into the country. Nature, Wallace says in "The Enjoyment of Nature," expands our consciousness; it is psychologically healing; and most important, by making us aware "of a distinct life within our being, of another world surrounding our universe," it leads us to the certitude of our spiritual essence.[11] Reminiscent at times in its phrasing of Emerson's concept of the over-soul, the article aroused the alarm of a correspondent who, under the name of "Clericus," accused its writer of pantheism and atheism.[12] It is not inconceivable that "Clericus" was Wallace himself. At any rate, in "A Dramatic Dream," "Clericus" comes to the editorial office, makes his charge, and receives the editor's careful distinction between a pantheist or materialist who worships nature and an "intense spiritualist" who sees in nature "only types and shadows and hieroglyphics" of God.[13]

In the same spirit, "Town and Country" presents a reconciled view toward the growth of the railroads, which not only bring people into the city but also take the urban population back to nature again.[14] "An Appeal to Women" associates the country with solitude, which liberates "the deeper inward emotions and aspirations" from the "tyranny of externality." Consequently, "fashion should undergo a complete interregnum during the summer." Late hours and "incessant gayety" have a fatal effect on "that downlike bloom of the spirit, which is, after all, the true talisman of a woman's fascination." In watering places like Newport and Saratoga, "a few women of established character and commanding influence" should "unite in breaking down the ab-surd, vulgar, and irksome system of dressing and visiting which is kept up by second-rate people for purposes of self-illustration and self-importance."[15] The same attitude dominates "Midsummer Madness," which compares the fashion mania that seized Newport in the summer of 1846 to the case of dancing madness occurring in the sixteenth century,[16] and "Newport, 1846," a celebration of the end of the summer season and emergence of "Old New-port—genuine, quiet, unostentatious, social Newport."[17]

Yet at other times Wallace can put up with the social whirl of his favorite resort, writing in "Summer Travel" that such watering places as Newport and Saratoga are no less unifying factors of American life than the railroads, bringing people from North, South, East, and West into "great national congresses on a social platform."[18] And "The Monarchy of Newport" affectionately advertises Newport's climate, scenery, and social pleasures. Even the "parvenus" are encouraged to come and display "their showy equipages."[19]

If the enjoyment of nature is beneficial to the quality of American life, so is the cultivation of art. "Every one," writes Wallace in "To Do—To Be," "is so occupied with the desire to *do*, that there is no leisure merely to *be:* accordingly at some periods of life, most persons have occasion to fulfill the other function of the verb, and *suffer*."[20] "American Enjoyments" blames "the undying instinct of self-advancement" in the American character—whether commercial or intellectual—for its enslaving properties.[21] Art, therefore, is recommended in several essays. "A New Gallery of Art" commends the advances America has already made in the cultivation of both the plastic arts and the opera, suggesting further that a great public gallery be established to possess good copies of great works, which are preferable to the purchasable, inferior originals of the masters.[22] Wallace meant primarily those of the Italian Renaissance. Dutch or Spanish painting was not yet fully appreciated at this time, and Wallace could not have foreseen what American wealth would be able to import from Europe in the next hundred years.

Wallace praises American artists in such articles as "Washington Allston"[23] and "Statuary in America,"[24] which touches on the work of Horatio Greenough and Hyram Powers. "The Education of Art" is interesting for what it reveals about Wallace's attitude toward music. "Of all the fine arts, music is the most sensuous and the least intellectual," he writes. "Except in rare instances, such as the harmonies of Beethoven, its relations with the more analytic powers of the mind are distant and feeble. . . . It refines the passions into sentiments, but it does not tend, as painting does, to raise the sentiments into ideas." Consequently, "the moral influences of the pencil are as healthy as those of music are morbid and extreme."[25] In a culture where musical taste found its highest expression in the Handel and Haydn Society of Boston; where Bach was almost unknown, Mozart thought chiefly charming, and Beethoven, although he had died in 1827, still approached gingerly because of his perplexing "harmonies"; such an attitude is not surprising. Nor does it reveal as much insensitivity to music on Wallace's part as a fear of emotion he cannot translate into concrete, or literal terms. The idea, of course, that music is a highly formalized language barely glimmers before him; and one wonders what he would have said about "ideas" in painting if confronted with abstract art.

In "Popular Education" he is on surer grounds, although in recommending more art education he is prone to stray into the popular American view that art is but an ornament.[26] Parks, as Wallace learned in Europe, can also be raised to the level of art; and in "Parks and Parking" he recalls the Tuilleries, Hampton Court, the Villa Borghese, and Schönbrunn, and recommends similar undertakings in American cities.[27] In "National Glory and the Arts" he recalls the munificence of Ludwig I of Bavaria and urges that the statues of important heroes of the American Revolution be erected in the rotunda of the Capitol. He would have exclaimed over the Statue of Liberty, though regretting perhaps that it did not portray Washington: "There ought to be upon the highest grounds of New York, upon the summit of a pillar visible widely over the waters, a figure which should announce to the European that he is about to tread the land of Washington."[28]

Many of Wallace's utterances on literature in the pages of the *Home Journal* attempt to elicit public interest. We have already noted "Plagiarism," with its special relevance to Poe, and "W. E. Channing," as a part of Wallace's review of Griswold's *Prose Writers of America*. Two interesting articles were to form parts of what might be called the notebook version of Wallace's review of Griswold's *Female Poets of America* (1849). "Female Authorship" notes the recent preponderance of women in literature, naming George Sand, Elizabeth Barrett, and Felicia Hemans among others.

Seeing literature as having progressed from "profound learning" to "liberty and nature," Wallace considers it in his own time as especially welcoming to "female genius."[29] In "Women and Literature" he speaks of the "mystic power" inherent in the concept of the Madonna, relating it in characteristic nineteenth-century manner to the particular "genuineness, chasteness, simplicity and virtue" of American literature brought about by the large number of women who form part of it.[30] Nearly half a century later, William Dean Howells would strike a similar note in his *Criticism and Fiction*.

"Honors to Literary Men," occasioned by Cooper's recent death, asks, "Why should we not have a Westminster Abbey—at least for literary men? Why would not Trinity serve for a Poet's Corner?"[31] In "Mr. Cooper and the Press" Wallace holds the press responsible for the general maligning of Cooper before his death, saying, "The press is a great power; but it is not the highest literary estate in the country!" Unless the press recognize its "limited rights" and "extensive duties—it will become an odious tyrant instead of a beneficient ruler."[32]

"An International Copyright" is a forceful plea against the wholesale importation of British books to the detriment of American writers.[33] The cry for an international copyright law was sounded by many, but it was not brought into existence until the Berne Convention of 1886. "American Literature" looks forward to the "development of a powerful national literature." The times are comparable in historical importance to those of Salamis and the defeat of the Armada, which echo in Aeschylus and Shakespeare, but American writers are still subservient to English and German models. "The self-dependent, strenuous, deeply-souled and widely-minded creator in letters has not yet risen among us . . . whose sympathies shall absorb the mighty, but as yet silent, inspiration with which the American is teeming, to reproduce it in vocal majesty and power."[34] The call in Emerson's "Poet," published two years previously, to which Whitman's *Leaves of Grass* (1855) was to be an answer, is echoed in these words. Whitman, who was editor of the *Brooklyn Eagle* at this time, may well have read them in the *National Press*.

Wallace's editorials touch on other aspects of American life. "The Railroads" is a plea for added comforts, as well as an attack on railroad monopolies,[35] a subject which Wallace was to develop, with special reference to the Camden and Amboy Railway monopoly in *Can the Monopoly Lawfully Be Abolished?*[36] "Railway Hints" is a series of specific suggestions based on European railroads: the carriages should be illuminated when passing through a tunnel, there should be first-class carriages, and regulations should assure the right of any passenger to close windows on the wind side.[37]

The defeat of Mexico in 1848 inspired Wallace in "War and its Conclusion" to state the American ideal: "Other governments conquer in order that they may subjugate, despoil, and tyrannize: we vanquish in order to elevate, improve, and bless."[38] We recall that, unlike Thoreau and other future abolitionists, Wallace had never been opposed to the Mexican War. One of the results of this war was the gold rush of 1849, and in "Emigration to California" Wallace warns that the price of gold, like any gift of nature, is labor.[39] His concern with the problems of government and politics is shown in "Legislation and its Systems," urging a minimum of legislation;[40] "The Presidency," calling for more dignified campaigning;[41] and "General Taylor's Cabinet," arguing for the appointment of Daniel Webster, who has made Whig victory possible by committing the Whigs to the Free-Soil Party, as Secretary of State. Without Webster, President Taylor's cabinet would be a "second-rate affair."[42]

As an observer of political events in France, Wallace argues in "De Lamartine" that this literary man "of genius, the brightest intelligence, and most elevated spirit perhaps in France," is nevertheless not the man for the presidency of the Second Republic.[43] The need is for a strong and resolute leader, Wallace asserts in "The Times and the Man," where he calls for a new Napoleon without mentioning Napoleon's nephew, whom he seems to mean.[44] Louis Napoleon's election and his subsequent seizure of dictatorial powers as Napoleon III was to demonstrate Wallace's conservative astuteness with a vengeance. The foreign policy Wallace proposes in "American Interference in European Politics" is an attempt to put into perspective Washington's warning against "entangling alliances." Washington would want America in the middle of the nineteenth century to exert a moral influence in the world. Specifically, whereas America has neither right nor duty to interfere with contending political parties within a state, when a state is struggling against "the abnormal, unreasonable, unnatural control and tyranny of a foreign nation," American intervention might be called for. For "the integrity and mutual independence of existing nations is a part of the public law of the world."[45]

Several of the editorials speak for America in her great mid-century rivalry with England. "Cockneyisms-Americanisms" asserts the existence of an American language, giving examples of words such as "sick," "luggage," and "clever" which have retained their Elizabethan or eighteenth-century usage in America but not in England.[46] The London Exhibition of 1851, of which Wallace sent a glowing report to the *Home Journal*,[47] occasioned the *London Times* to ridicule the paltriness of American manufacture; and in "The Great Exhibition of 1851" Wallace places the blame on a lack of preparation in America, whereby tradesmen were allowed to send second-rate products to London primarily for commercial purposes.[48] America regained much of her prestige that summer, when the yacht *The America* took first prize on August 22 at the international contest at Cowes. "We offer our compliments to 'The Times' on the subject," Wallace exulted in "The America at Cowes."[49] The British press spoke of the victory patronizingly as an achievement of the Anglo-Saxon race, and Wallace replied in a letter to the *Home Journal* by saying that "it is to the infusion of blood in our veins that is *not* Anglo-Saxon . . . that we owe our superiority to England," and signed himself "O'Brian."[50] British claims to the invention of the telegraph were answered by Wallace in two articles. "American Society and Science" associates American unification with American inventive genius in three important fields: locomotion (Fulton and Stevens), printing (Hoe), and electricity (Franklin, Henry, and Morse).[51] "England, America, and Prof. Morse" reminds England of her tendency to piracy throughout history, concluding that Morse's name "will stand forever as a monument of the ingenuity of America and the dishonest jealousy of England."[52]

As might be expected, finding an article in *Fraser's Magazine* which asked in what sense Hiram Powers's *Greek Slave* was Greek made Wallace gasp. "The *insensibility* displayed in this paragraph," he writes in "Powers' Greek Slave," "to the spiritual and moral, and the capacity to perceive only the physical, can hardly be paralleled."[53] For this statue, which is thought of today as a pleasing minor work of the Romantic pseudo-Classical school, was for Wallace a great deal more. Partaking of the literalist art criticism of the age, he was keenly interested in the psychological revelation of the work as "an expression of offended dignity." Its near nudity, which raised some Victorian eyebrows, was also an aspect for an enlightened mind to defend. Finally, it was an American work. Nothing could have delighted Wallace more than

to be able to report in "The Great Exhibition" that Queen Victoria
and her little entourage sat one morning for more than half an hour
in front of it.[54]

III *Book and Drama Reviews*

Compared to the analytical book reviews familiar today, those of
the mid-nineteenth century often seem two-dimensional, with an
overuse of both superlatives and invectives. But it must be borne in
mind that before the days of large, dramatic book ads and book
clubs, reviews served promotional ends to a far greater extent than
they do today; whereas on the negative side they tended to become
a vehicle for various forms of animosity.

Wallace's motives for his positive reviews, which appeared mainly in the *National Press-Home Journal*, were frequently personal.
We have already examined the elaborate review he constructed for
Griswold's *Prose Writers of America* and have touched on those he
wrote for some of Griswold's other projects. Although Wallace
reviewed James D. Nourse's *Remarks on the Past*[55] on George P.
Morris's recommendation, the glowing ten-page review of this
young and relatively unknown historian's work, complete with extensive quotations, which took the *Home Journal* two installments
to print, reveals much sincere enthusiasm. Wallace's high praise of
Emily Chubbuck's ("Fanny Forester") *Trippings in Author-Land*[56]
is largely the result of their friendship. Relating the author's talents
to the upsurge of female authorship, the review manages to pay a
compliment to Madame de Stael as a luminary in the field. Similarly, Wallace's comments on Fitz-Greene Halleck[57] pay tribute not
only to the author of "Bozzaris" and "Alnwick Castle," which
rekindle the "enthusiasms of youth," but to poetry in general.
Whether Wallace knew Lydia Peirson we do not know, but his effusions over her "voice from the forest"[58] suggest that he did, or
perhaps that he felt that she was being unjustly attacked. The personal element in the review of Jacob Randolph's *Memoir on . . .
Philip Syng Physick, M.D.*[59] is directed not to the author but to the
subject, whom Wallace gratefully remembers. This review oc-
casions Wallace to recognize two types of human genius: one
"whose intellectual action is of an electrical kind—instant, intense
and momentary," and another, whose "accumulation of mental
energy is given forth with the gradual, steady and continuous flow
of galvanic current" (*LC*, 57). Wallace judges both to be "equally

divine," which is interesting to set beside Poe's narrower dictum: "The ordinary talk about 'continuous and sustained effort' is pure twaddle and nothing more. Perseverance is one thing and genius is another" (*Works*, XIII, 152). Another passage that is of particular interest to any student of Wallace himself is his call for a full-length biography of Dr. Physic, even though as a man of "extreme sensibilities" Physic was "unwilling that his private letters and papers should be laid before the public." For "it has been doubted by many how far . . . the commands of the dead should operate when the interests of society are in question" (*LC*, 58).

A number of Wallace's reviews are laudatory without any personal element. Enchanted by Motte-Fouqué's novel, *Undine*,[60] Wallace points to the success with which the realistic and fantastic elements have been "not wrought . . . but cast" into a homogeneous whole—an accomplishment that he feels is lacking in some greater works, like *The Tempest*. In reviewing Lord Mahon's edition of Chesterfield's *Letters to his Son*,[61] Wallace is impressed with Chesterfield's practicality, which he is careful to tell us must not be confused with principle at a theoretical level. Emancipated from Dr. Johnson's famous strictures of Chesterfield, yet writing in a Victorian milieu, Wallace gingerly and cleverly steers his course by interpreting the Earl's advice to his son to have an intrigue with any woman of high fashion as an anxious parent's strategy: "If he passes the evening with a lady of *ton*, he loses his virtue, it is true; but if I do not send him to such a woman, he will certainly go himself to one of the lower sort, where, besides his virtue, he will lose his character and impair his manners to boot" (*LC*, 132).

The Rev. Joseph Spence's *Anecdotes*,[62] a book mainly about Pope, receives Wallace's favorable comments with a view to American publication, but there is no record that it ever appeared here. More interesting is his review of Basil Montague's selections from Taylor, Barrow, Fuller, and others, which appeared in *Wiley and Putnam's Library of Choice Reading* series.[63] Condemning the recent flood of cheap editions as impermanent both physically and in content, Wallace praises the Wiley and Putnam series, whose volumes are cheap yet well made and bring works of high quality to the reader. He feels the present volume is of value in making its selections from authors "who have five lines well worth remembering among five hundred scarce worth reading" (*LC*, 145).

Wallace's review of the *Memoirs* of Oliver Wolcott, Secretary of the Treasury under Hamilton,[64] is written in the spirit of his deeply

felt Federalism. The characters and actions of such men as
Washington and John Adams must be studied so as to "raise, expand and purify" present-day politics. Wallace expressed himself in
private correspondence, too, on Wolcott's *Memoirs*, making the
suggestion that a fund be established for the publication of the
papers of early statesmen (*LC*, 66 - 67). He went so far as to draw
up a "Protocol" (*LC*, 458 - 60), but there is no record that he ever
put his plan into practice.

Favorable reviews of lesser importance include one on the
autobiography of Blanco White, member of the Oxford Movement
and author of the fine sonnet "On Night," which Coleridge praised
highly.[65] In his review of Sidney Smith's sermons,[66] Wallace finds
occasion to say that many contemporary preachers—in contrast to
Smith's fine sense of humor—"begin by insulting the understanding . . . proceed by wakening and exasperating every dormant
prejudice . . . and they end with leaving those errors, which they
attack by so mad a strategy, entrenched in pride, and fortified by
passion" (*LC*, 154 - 55). In his review of Carlyle's *Critical and
Miscellaneous Essays*,[67] Wallace admires Carlyle's "intolerance of
cant" and his skepticism, although he does not rank him as a first-
rate intellect.

Among Wallace's unfavorable reviews the harshest one is that of
Frederick von Raumer's *America and the American People*.[68]
Foreign critics of American life, writing with characteristic foreign
prejudice and superficiality of observation, did not amuse Wallace.
Raumer's book was hailed as a thorough and wise book, but
Wallace found it dull, reminding him of a huge mathematical
equation reducible to zero. He is irritated over Raumer's statistics
on the Americans' spitting habits and over his shallow lauding of
"Washington, Jefferson, Adams, and Jackson, as men of the same
stamp, differing in the degree of their republican feelings, but not
in the nature of their political views" (*LC*, 120). "Rubio's"
*Rambles in the United States and in Canada during the Summer of
1845*[69] evokes from him the following:

We are not pleased at the re-publication of these works; they fester
wounds that should be permitted to heal, and sow dissentions between
nations that should be friends. At the same time that we make this remark,
we cannot but express an earnest hope that we may live to see the day
when Americans shall mentally acknowledge a conscientious standard of
their own, and learn to treat with laughter and contempt the petty attacks
made through ignorance or envy of our institutions, and fear at our increasing power and commanding position. (*LC*, 164)

Further unfavorable reviews include that of Horace Walpole's *Memoirs of the Reign of King George the Third*,[70] which Wallace calls "a series of outrageous libels." He is disturbed by the mixture of Toryism and radicalism in Dr. Thomas Arnold, whose *Introductory Lectures on Modern History*[71] seems to him the work of an enthusiast to be approached with "guarded interest and suspecting admiration." George Gilfillan's *Sketches of Modern Literature*,[72] a discussion of twenty-six important contemporary literary figures, seems to have been at least useful, but Wallace found it worthless. About the popular Martin Tupper[73] he is similarly disparaging, calling his art a contrivance not of thoughts but "things that look like thoughts." His comments on the anonymous Quaker pamphlet, *The Legal Rights of Woman*,[74] is an embarrassing reminder that notwithstanding his enthusiastic reception of women authors, he did not carry his feminism very far. Whereas it is proper, he argues here, that a wife should be protected by law against the husband's misfortunes, it is wrong that she should seek legal protection against the husband, who is the only source of her safety.

It will be in order here to refer to Wallace's article on Washington Irving, although it stands somewhat apart from these reviews because of its length and range. When, apparently through Griswold, Wallace sold it to *Sartain's Union Magazine* he received for it the relatively large sum of forty dollars.[75] It is a thorough and honest work, among the best of Wallace's critical writings. Wallace's affection for the writer who did much for the recognition of American literature abroad is present in every page, yet the criticism is uncompromising. The article first names some of Irving's virtues such as his pervading pleasantness, his restraint, and "the subdued key to which everything is pitched." The single failure in Irving, says Wallace, is that he is content with fancy; in terms of Coleridge's distinction,

in an imaginative view of a scene, the mental consciousness of the person, or the moral character of the occasion, reacts upon the outward scene with such overpowering and transfusing energy that all things around become but types and symbols—nay, the very complements and visible parts—of that which is within. You behold the scene not as it is but as it is felt or as it appears . . . in a speculum of thought or passion already warped or colored by the master emotion. (*LC*, 74)

Irving's fancy, in contrast, is illustrated by a passage from "The Legend of Sleepy Hollow," in which Ichabod Crane is about to encounter the Headless Horseman. "It was the very witching time of night," Irving writes, and Wallace comments:

The mast, which should have appeared as a strange, gleaming thing, weird and spectral, raising indefinite apprehensions, becomes a familiar and calming sight by being referred to a sloop "riding quietly at anchor under the land." The distant bay of the watch-dog is well managed; but the drowsy crowing of the cock, which might with great effect have been made to have mysterious relation to the return of wandering ghosts to their sepulchral tenements, is brought back to quotidian unmeaningness by being made to proceed from a bird "accidentally awakened." . . . Compare all this with one of Shakespeare's nights! Mr. Irving's failure in this case is to be ascribed to defect of imagination, and consequent excess of inappropriate and discordant detail. (LC, 77)

In Irving's descriptions Wallace sees "the original and model" for Dickens. But, although "Mr. Irving is an exquisite delineator of external manners," he "has no power of representing character" (LC, 80). Irving has both narrative power and humor, but his humor is again fanciful, rather than imaginative: "Quaint, droll, comic—what you will, in the line of diverting, laughter-moving conceit—we can scarcely admit his possession of that grand, deep pathetic, meditative inspiration, Humor—a faculty which seems to be the combination and the key of all our nature's sympathies" (LC, 82).

Among Irving's writing Wallace prefers, as do modern critics, *The Sketch Book. Bracebridge Hall*, he says, is artificial; *The History of New York* carries humor to overworked lengths. *Columbus* is first-rate narration but too fictional to be good history; *The Conquest of Granada* carries this fault even further: "We feel as if the chronicler was trifling with us. The essence of romance is poured out in such profusion as to become sickening." And he asserts again that *The Sketch Book* "is the perfect flower of all of Irving's faculties" (LC, 89).

Wallace's comments on the drama have come down in eight pieces. Some of these are general articles, others are specific reviews. In "Decline of the Drama," written in 1844 but published in the *Home Journal* only seven years later,[76] Wallace advances the dubious theory that the opera and drama "have never flourished together." "The Regular Drama"[77] is a conventional argument for the theater as a cultural institution. In his review of Charles Kean's Othello at the Philadelphia production in the fall of 1845,[78]

Wallace is impressed by Kean's portrayal of the reawakening in the Moor of the "slumbering sympathies of a savage origin. . . . He is passion-struck; the intellect has sunk. . . . He reverences and follows the mental lead of Iago, as a savage worships his *Fetiche*" (*LC*, 455 -56). Wallace bestows high praise on Kean's wife, Ellen Tree, for her portrayal of Desdemona, confessing that she has shaken his previous views, based on a William Macready production, which were "unfavorable to the delicacy and perfect integrity of Desdemona's character" (*LC*, 455). Wallace's personal enchantment with Ellen Tree becomes fully expressed in two separate articles about her, one a specific review of her Rosalind in *As You Like It*.[79]

But he ultimately prefers Macready's more intellectual interpretations—which give us "a grander impression even of the genius of Shakespeare himself"—to the Keans' more passionate ones.[80] In his review of Macready's Macbeth, he is particularly impressed by Macready's portrayal of Macbeth's rejection of conscience after Duncan's murder, in order to remove "the natural pain resulting from inconsistency between one's principles and one's acts"; and Macbeth's hardening of heart after the ghost scene. "Here the voice of the actor changes—his manner for the future is decided and firm; from the slave he has become the hero of wickedness. In the three first acts, almost as sensitive as Hamlet, in the two last he is almost as ruthless as Richard. Yet still, his ferocity is very distinguishable from 'the hardness by long habitude produced' of the misshapen son of York. His vigor is passion; his severity is impulse; his courage is the frenzy of shame" (*LC*, 447 - 48).

In "Prospects of the Drama,"[81] written last in the series, Wallace greets the coming season of 1848 - 49 as the most promising one in the last twelve years, little knowing that it would be marked by the eruption of the rivalry between Edwin Forrest and William Macready on May 10, 1849, in the notorious Astor Place riot in New York, with a toll of thirty-one people killed and one hundred-fifty wounded. Wallace names Forrest, Macready, Charles Kemble and his daughter Fanny (Mrs. Butler) among those scheduled to appear on the stage, but he warns that the star system, which has caused the break-down of the stock companies, must be supplanted by greater rotation of roles and consequent development of good supporting casts.

CHAPTER 5

Art and Scenery

I *Aesthetic Principles*

ALWAYS sensitive to beauty and concerned with art—and
seemingly the author of an unpublished book on architecture—Wallace rounded out his art education during the year that
he spent in Europe in 1850 - 51. He writes,

> My own preparation for these studies had been slight, and my appreciation
> of them was of course limited, yet I can scarcely now write upon the sub-
> ject without falling into the language of enthusiasm. I am sure the canons
> of the Cathedral of Parma concluded me lunatic, when they saw me
> stretched upon my back for hours, under the incomparable Assumption by
> Correggio in their cupola. And it was with what I might, without exaggera-
> tion, call a rational delirium of pleasure that I viewed through successive
> hours the Madonna di San Sisto at Dresden, and the Madonna della
> Misericordia at Lucca.[1]

His notebook entries, some of which appear to have been further
revised, have come down in the first posthumous collection of his
writings, *Art, Scenery and Philosophy in Europe*, where they
assured the high regard in which Wallace would be held by his surviving contemporaries as a writer on art. Wallace's aesthetic principles are contained largely in the four essays that head this collection. In general, his views reflect the idealism of such recent
aestheticians as Schelling and Hegel,[2] although it is not certain
whether he read their works. Specifically, Wallace subscribes fully
to Hegel's doctrine that art is not an imitation of nature but an expression of the ideal; furthermore he recognizes the role of
religious impulse in artistic creation, as does Hegel. But just as important is the fact that he does not follow Hegel into the famous
corollary of his thought, according to which art develops through
three succeeding stages: architecture, which is symbolic; sculpture,

114

which is classical; and painting, which is romantic. Wallace might have read Hegel, but he was intent through these essays on working out his own aesthetic.

"Art, an Emanation of Religious Affection" is an attempt to define the rare human faculty involved in the creation of art, which Wallace sees as "single, distinct, original, and natural" (*ASE*, 4). As it is the special gift of certain individuals, so collectively it is the special gift of certain historical periods. Nor is "Art" equally applicable to all modes of creative expression. Its special character is best shown by architecture, sculpture, and painting. Literature is too intellectual, music too sensuous "to admit that perfect balance of the elements of the sensible and thoughtful . . . which art requires" (*ASE*, 5). Considering the greatest examples of art to be Greek sculpture and architecture, Gothic architecture, and Italian painting, Wallace concludes that "the art-faculty is nothing else than earnest religious feeling acting imaginatively, or imagination working under the elevating and kindling influences of religious feeling" (*ASE*, 6).

One may object on a number of grounds. The intellectual aspect of music, not to speak of its profoundly religious possibilities, seems to have escaped Wallace again, as it did in previous writings. Clearly, he defines "intellectual" and "sensuous" inadequately, on the strength of his subjective response to certain works of art. His supportive argument holds up with respect to Gothic architecture, which is the product of a tremendous wave of religious feeling; but it falters with respect to Italian painting, which reached the stage he most admires not when religious life was most intense in Italy but some three centuries later, at a time of relative secularism. And with reference to the Greeks, he is obliged to stretch the meaning of "religious feeling" to include the Greeks' instinctive "adoration" of "the personality of man." Yet as we wish that Wallace had begun by choosing some other criterion for classifying the arts—perhaps spatial and temporal organization, or types of perception—we are bound to admire the attempt itself, the tremendous concern with beauty, which was rare in America in the middle of the nineteenth century. We are bound also to commend Wallace for his insistence that art is more than mere imitation—a concept with which Western civilization was cursed until the time of Hegel, thanks to Plato and Aristotle.

Wallace bases his second essay, called appropriately "Art, Sym-

bolic, not Imitative," on the pre-Hegelian theory that sees the
three historical stages of art as archaic, perfect, and in decline.
Once again Wallace points to religious feeling as an essential element in art, but here he broadens its definition to include "the interior meaning to be communicated or represented." The fervor of
this "interior meaning" in the archaic stage is illustrated by a
passage strikingly modern in tone:

The fondness in children and savages for drawing and modeling belongs to
the general system of *Expression*. Every feeling, every sentiment, every
thought in man impulsively tends to outwardness or utterance; for these all
are agitations of the interior life which are propagated towards the exterior
organs. . . . Imagination is then [in children] so overpowerful that
figurative apprehension prevails entirely over sensible perception, and the
dreams that form their inward life work themselves out in visionary scenes
through symbols formed from familiar articles by the typifying energy of
their conceptions. (*ASE*, 22)

In the second, or perfect, stage religious fervor subsides into
"earnest sentiment . . . capable of entering into union with purely natural forms in an idealized state, and of being completely
carried and explained by them" (*ASE*, 23). Finally in the decline,
"all religious motive vanishes," and art forgets "its prophetic and
mediatorial function and merely reflects the dull actual" (*ASE*, 23).
Wallace goes on to cite examples from various periods, expanding his range to include Etruscan and Egyptian, as well as
Chinese and Indian art. Some of his assertions are dubious; he
tends, for example, to see the development of Western art too
much as a continuous process. But the essay is eminently readable,
its author's familiarity with art revealing far more than one year of
study. One of Wallace's important points is that the current interest in landscape painting is an unmistakable manifestation of the
decline. He may be replying to Ruskin, whose *Modern Painters*
had begun to appear in 1843. Wallace ends his essay with the
pronouncement that the art of his day "is smitten with incurable
barrenness" (*ASE*, 38), and the reader is left to wonder whether in
the far more interesting art of the next hundred years Wallace
would have seen the archaic stage of a new cycle.
"The Law of the Development of Gothic Architecture" is a
demonstration of the functionalist proposition that in
art—specifically in Gothic architecture—"the spirit came first, and
not the forms; and the spirit created the forms which it required for

its uses" (*ASE*, 40). Thus it is futile to search for the first oc-
currence of the pointed arch in order to mark the beginning of the
Gothic form, which was an outgrowth of the Romanesque, which in
turn was an outgrowth of Roman ruins. Wallace believes that the
first time the Gothic spirit manifested itself was in the Norman
architecture around Caen, although the arches employed were still
round, and that from there it went to England to work out its own
development there. Modern art historians tend to agree. Wallace
believes that the pointed arch was first suggested by two round
arches intersecting, and since the new form suited the creative impulse it was employed and refined by builders more and more extensively. It is equally jejune, Wallace argues, to credit any one
country with the full flowering of the Gothic. Through copious examples he shows that "individuals in different places and
successive times are the organs of certain progressions and im-
provements in the Art, which, when viewed together, are found to
have a systematic connection that the separate agents neither knew
nor intended" (*ASE*, 52).

As Wallace warms to his subject, his reliance on evolutionary
thought, which filled the air before its climactic expression in
Darwin's *Origin of Species* in 1859, is all the more apparent. He
speaks of the "vital force" of Gothic architecture containing "a
constant principle or impulse of progression and evolution," which
results in a "successive reproduction of the style under a modified
variety." He calls this process "one of the most important laws of
Art." For "when there is no continuous progression, in better or
worse taste, but merely stagnation or capricious and unconnected
shootings in this or that direction, the life of Art is gone" (*ASE*,
52 - 53). And by way of a brilliant illustration, he turns to the London Parliament House, "one of the most boasted structures of
modern times":

Grandiose in dimensions and gorgeous in decorations, it shows not one ray
of invention. . . . It resembles a cast-iron stove on a great scale, or a cast-
iron railing in which a commonplace form is repeated insipidly without
modification. Chartres or Ely is a tree, growing freely and boldly, en-
countering obstacles, and surmounting or working them in with an energy
that makes deviation a new and higher illustration of principle. (*ASE*, 54 -
55)

In his fragmentary "Principle of Beauty in Works of Art,"
Wallace gives new emphasis to the concept of usefulness. For as

nature is idealized in painting and sculpture, so, correspondingly, use is idealized in architecture. The Parthenon, for example, is ultimately reducible to the cottage. Similarly, "the cathedral, in its general form and arrangement, is not a fanciful contrivance; it is but an imaginative expansion and modification of the Basilica, which had been framed for utility and convenience" (*ASE*, 62). Effect in this respect is important—the spiritual use to which certain formal elements are put. Thus in the cathedral, "while the pier was a single cylinder, there was a complete break, and even opposition between its plain roundness and the multitudinous arches that rose from it. To obviate this, each arch, above, was furnished with its own small column" to carry the eye uninterruptedly upward. "Again, the exquisite rib vaulting and groining of the ceilings, is a mere display of the actual principles upon which the building is held up" (*ASE*, 62 - 63). Drawing a sharp contrast to the spirit of functionalism, Wallace refers to the Roman arch, "which brought in a new principle of construction and support; yet in apparent effect the Greek style was adhered to. Hence all became imposture. The arch was concealed; false entablatures were fabricated; and as the true elements of the building could not be shown, to form a basis of decoration, ornaments wholly foreign and fanciful were heaped on" (*ASE*, 61).

Writing in the *Literary History of the United States*, Willard Thorp calls some of these ideas by Wallace "far in advance of his time."[3] More specifically, Thorp recognizes Wallace as "one of the first to propose a functional theory of architecture," alluding, it seems, to Horatio Greenough, whom he discusses a dozen pages previously. While in Florence, Wallace visited Greenough,[4] and the two men probably exchanged ideas. But Wallace's functionalism is far more theoretical than the functionalism of Greenough, whose essays, which appeared in the year of Wallace's death,[5] show a greater concern with the problem of developing a suitable type of architecture for America. At any rate, from opposing points of emphasis, both men anticipated Louis Sullivan's famous dictum that function determines form, by some fifty years.

II *Cathedrals and Great Paintings*

In considering Wallace's application of his aesthetic principles, it is important to understand the state of art criticism in the middle of the nineteenth century. Modern formal analysis had made only a gentle stir.[6] In painting and sculpture the emphasis was on subject matter and its evocation of idea and feeling; thus John Ruskin could write in 1843 of Turner's *Slave Ship* in such terms as these: "The fire of the sunset falls along the trough of the sea, dyeing it with an awful but glorious light, the intense and lurid splendor which burns like gold and bathes like blood."[7] In architecture, as we might expect, formal considerations were forced on the writer somewhat more readily.

Wallace's "Cathedrals of the Continent" is a series of critical descriptions. Surprisingly, neither Chartres nor Notre Dame of Paris, nor any of the English cathedrals is among the fifteen represented, whereas there is a heavy concentration on the less interesting German structures. Possibly Wallace intended eventually to expand the series.

Frequently the descriptions are detailed and objective. Of the cathedral at Reims, for example, Wallace writes in the following manner: "The whole of the face below the towers is arranged in three grades or stories. The wide base is composed of, apparently, five arched portals, under crooked canopies or pediments, forming together a kind of frame which rises pyramidically in the center . . ." (*ASE*, 65 - 66). No doubt he understood perfectly that no verbal account can replace the act of seeing; it seems that some of his painstaking descriptions were rather an aid to his own careful observation and were intended to perform a similar service for the reader.

The critical passages are always more interesting. Of the sculpture on the façade of Reims, Wallace says, showing an understanding of the medieval builders' problem of relating sculpture to architecture,

To me it is less agreeable, because less natural and consistent than the method, more common in England, and to be found in the earlier buildings of France, which uses purely architectural forms of geometric characters. But since statuary was to be largely employed—according to the type then prevalent—its *assimilation* with the organic outlines of the compass and square, in the present case, certainly shows great knowledge and a mastering genius. (*ASE*, 66)

Consequently, Wallace welcomes the open spaces of the towers and parts of the façade under them that "ventilate, as it were, the holy crowd" and "interrupt that oppressiveness which such a dense multitude even of the saintly and apostolic humanity might have caused" (*ASE*, 67).

He is moved by the power of the western rose window of Reims—"a vast wheel filled with glass of scarlet and green"—but he gives higher praise to the interior of Bourges (St. Étienne), whose architect had "the deep, and accurate, and fearless genius" of discarding the transcepts. "The cross form is, in my judgment, inappropriate in Gothic architecture. Its proper employment is in connection with the dome, as in the Byzantine and Italian structures. . . . The characteristic effect of Gothic consists in developing long continuous vistas of arched avenues, and the transcept only breaks and defeats this impression" (*ASE*, 74). Would he give up, one might object, the marvelous surprise, as one proceeds forward in the nave, of the transcepts with their rose windows suddenly looming into view—since mystery is another Gothic characteristic? His position is nevertheless well argued by the example he gives of the cathedral of Siena, whose architect "felt the evil and labored to defeat it" by continuing the vaulting of the nave and aisles, including the triforium gallery, right through the transcepts, with the result that these are "reduced to truncated arms cut off and dangling uselessly at the sides" (*ASE*, 75).

An interesting example of Wallace's taste is his dissatisfaction with the supposed perfection of Amiens. Of the interior he says,

There is nothing that severe taste can condemn; indeed everything that it must admire. The altitude particularly is glorious. Yet altogether it fails to excite much enthusiasm. It wants character and expression. Its monotonous regularity and uniformity make it more an illustration of the rules of architecture than an embodiment of the spirit of Art. I find not in it those daring outbreaks of creative power, those unconscious workings out of deep sentiments . . . in which the conventional outlines of the science become subordinate to absorbing influences of special genius; which I do see in Tours, and Rheims, and Bourges. (*ASE*, 81)

In Tours, for example,

the nave seems like a long avenue leading into the church, which might seem to begin with the transcepts and choir. Such an arrangement, however, would have caused the nave to appear too narrow, were it not for the great height and width of the side aisles, which come to the relief of the true nave, and the adjacent chapels, which produce a great expansion and restore to the body of the church that pre-eminence of grandeur which it ought to possess over the choir. (*ASE*, 85)

Wallace points to the "absolute unity between the towers and the façade" in Strasbourg; but he feels that the finest tower in Europe is that of Freiburg-im-Breisgau because of "the great height of the open lantern which mediates and interprets" between the tower and the spire, as well as the "lofty and slender lightness" of the spire itself. "I tore myself away with the reluctance of a lover from this captivating form of beauty; and I shall always retain a conviction that there is one perfect thing in the world—the tower and spire of Friburg Cathedral" (*ASE*, 98).

In the cathedral at Milan, the superimposition of Gothic elements on a basic Greek design leads Wallace to observe, "It is a monster perhaps according to the botany of architecture, but it is like the peerless and perfect rose . . . and we may grant pardon to a deviation which works out an affluence of charms that bewilders the mind in admiration and makes faint the sense with delight" (*ASE*, 109).

Milan leads the reader tonally, as well as geographically, to the climax of the series, which is St. Peter's in Rome. Wallace dwells on the various approaches to "that great, dazzling structure," whose dome, however, when observed from the slopes of Tivoli, can also loom against the bright horizon "black, weird, portentious" (*ASE*, 113 - 14). In the interior, he is most interested in the architectural problem of making physical magnitude appear smaller in order to make it "familiar and conciliating" to the observer, which he believes to have been the joint effort of Michelangelo, Raphael, and Bramante. Mere size in distant objects, he believes, makes for a distinctness that brings them closer; this principle is augmented in St. Peter's by "a great diversity of rich and warm coloring . . . over the distant surfaces of airy cupolas and the retiring nooks of wall and ceiling." Moreover, "where the vault of the nave springs from the side piers, the upward lines are broken by a heavy, terminating cornice and by a broad transverse architrave; and further to baffle and expel all possibility of continuity with the marbled and fluted pilasters, the ceiling is composed of small, richly gilded panels. The width of the nave and aisles is also exceedingly great so as to bring down the height" (*ASE*, 119).

Against the opinion of many travelers who have found their first glimpse of the interior of St. Peter's disappointing, Wallace asserts, "You are not overpowered, bowed down, abased in terror or in tears, as you are upon going into almost the meanest of the English cathedrals," with their Protestant spirit, which was unconsciously at work in the North even before the Reformation. Catholicism "brings down heaven to man" (*ASE*, 119 - 22).

The "literary" approach that characterized art criticism in the nineteenth century makes Wallace's "Remarks upon Painters" a less interesting series. Nor does it often exhibit the critical spirit that emboldened Wallace to attack the whole idea of transcepts or to call the regularity of Amiens monotonous. By 1851, Ruskin had made his momentous pronouncement in favor of the pre-Raphaelites,[8] a factor that makes Wallace's exclusive concern with the five painters of the high Rennaissance he treats here especially conservative.

Among them, Michaelangelo "dwells supreme." In his work, physical size and strength always represent spiritual grandeur. His creations are effortless, and he likes to represent power in repose. An interesting example is his frequent bending of the hand inward at the wrist, which, incidentally, becomes a "tedious mannerism" in Vasari and other imitators. But Michelangelo's portrayal of spiritual grandeur does not preclude tenderness, sensibility, and sympathy. "From him we learn that nothing is so touching as the repressed softness of strong, great souls" (*ASE*, 220). In the Sistine Chapel, Wallace comments on eleven of the twelve prophets and sybils, speaking of Jeremiah, for example, as "thoughtful, absorbed and wrapt, yet quick in every fibre with the ethereal fire of pervading inspiration" (*ASE*, 221). But surprisingly he says nothing about the famous *Creation of Adam* on the ceiling; and it is not until he comes to discuss the *Holy Family* at the Uffizi in Florence that he notes Michelangelo's sculpturesque quality—an observation basic to the modern critic.

Coming to Leonardo da Vinci, Wallace notes that his emphasis in painting the human face is not on expression, which is fleeting, but on character, which allows the face to become "the soul's confessional" (*ASE*, 231). That Wallace had access to Leonardo's writings is doubtful, so that it is interesting to note the similarity of his observation to Leonardo's own statement: "A good painter has two chief objects to paint—man and the intention of his soul."[9] Wallace regrets that the "dogmatizing scepticism" of recent German critics has cast doubt on the authenticity of several paintings long attributed to Leonardo. He makes a half-hearted attempt to argue that in certain paintings which were being newly attributed to Luini, for example, "the mighty soul of Leonardo is to be traced through every part of the design," but he is aware that he cannot withhold the philological tide. Among other works, *Mona Lisa* only "seems" to Wallace by Leonardo, yet significantly he comments on it with particular intensity: "The face is serene and undisturbed, yet strong as Fate: soft and unintense, yet inevitable and irresistible. Its glance seems to follow you about the room like an embodied conscience. It gazes upon you in still, cold sovereignty, as if it possessed all the secrets of your soul" (*ASE*, 236). Twenty years later, Pater would add, as it were, "Like the vampire, she has been dead many times and learned the secrets of the grave."[10] The authenticity of the *Last Supper*—made world-famous through Rafaello Morghen's engraving—seems to Wallace beyond dispute. He takes a long, melancholy look at the present ruined condition of this work, "upon which rests Leonardo's claim to take a place among the greatest painters of the world" (*ASE*, 237).

In turning to a lesser figure, Wallace becomes in some ways more interesting, certainly more critical. He calls Fra Bartolomeo, Leonardo's pupil, "the most spiritual of perfect artists"; but he "represents spirituality not in the metaphysical, notional abstractness of Fra Beato, but as embodied in character and life" (*ASE*, 240). Some of Bartolomeo's figures show "a somewhat square type of skull," some of his faces "an anxious, unhappy look characteristic of the imagination of an ascetic and monastic recluse." He is a master of drapery, yet is sometimes tempted into a "profuse and cumbersome display of it"; his colors, although soft and brilliant "in a mellow and juicy style," show the "thinness and flare" of the Florentine, rather than the "solidity, truth, or perfect harmony" of the Venetian school. Among Bartolomeo's works, Wallace considers the *Madonna della Misericordia* in the Church of San Romano in Lucca the greatest. His lengthy and painstaking description of this work begins with a noteworthy anticipation of formalistic criticism through a series of such terms as "composition," "color," "chiaroscuro," and "unity of effect" (*ASE*, 244). Wallace is aware of the mutual influence between Bartolomeo and the somewhat younger Raphael (recent critics state more precisely that Bartolomeo taught color, composition, and drapery to Raphael and learned perspective from him), and, notwithstanding his previous stance against "dogmatizing scepticism," he calls here for greater scholarly precision in dating works of art (*ASE*, 250).

In his essay on Perugino, Wallace suggests the interesting theory that an ancient marble group of the Graces, dug up at Siena in the

thirteenth century, may have provided a model for Perugino, his
pupil Raphael, and their school. The specific work Wallace seems
to mean is Raphael's *Three Graces*, whose source, however, recent
critics ascribe to a medal by Niccolo di Forzore Spinelli, rather than
the ancient group.[11] On the basis, at any rate, of a classical sculp-
tural quality in Perugino, Raphael, and their followers, Wallace
separates them from the Florentines, as modern critics separate
them on the basis of their spatial organization.[12] The ultimate
source of all Italian painting is of course Giotto, whose importance
Wallace fully recognizes by calling his style "the reservoir from
which through various channels were led the rivulets that fed the
Perugian, Florentian, and Venetian schools" (*ASE*, 252). Wallace is
especially interested here in Perugino's position as Raphael's
teacher. Although Raphael was in no sense Perugino's imitator, he
"*originated* none of those forms of the Virgin and child with which
his immortality is associated. He only added that nature and vitality to the forms of Perugino which were required to bring them to
perfection." Hence, "some, not a considerable portion, of the fame
of Raphael justly belongs to Perugino" (*ASE*, 260).

Wallace seems to be using "form" in a more modern sense in the
next essay, which is unfinished yet decidedly the most dynamic of
the group, where he calls Raphael "a creator of perfect forms"
(*ASE*, 268). In contrast to Michelangelo's greater intellectual content—which modern critics see as greater passion—Wallace calls
Raphael "more effectually an artist." One need not agree, but the
statement is consistent with the Romantic critics' inordinate
emphasis of subject matter. Wallace recognizes three types of
Raphael madonnas: those mainly symbolizing motherhood, those
attempting an historical representation, and those emphasizing the
Virgin's doctrinal character. Of the last group is the *Sistine Madonna* in Dresden, which he praises highly. He is less enthusiastic
about the unfinished *Transfiguration* in the Vatican, which leads
him to say—in a spirit counter to his assertion above—that "the
Corregiesque power of fusing all elements together in one burning
whole" was not Raphael's. "The perspective effect appears to me
to fail utterly. The chiaro-scuro is decidedly bad" (*ASE*, 290). Nor
is he enthusiastic about two large-scale works that have been greatly esteemed recently for their sense of rhythm, *School of Athens*
and *Disputa*, also in the Vatican. Yet when Wallace calls their composition "somewhat cold, lifeless, and heavy" (*ASE*, 279), one must
note that the recent art historian Adolfo Venturi speaks in a similar

vein of the "greater warmth" Raphael had yet to learn after their completion.[13]

Wallace goes on to consider a group of late portraits, including one of Pope Leo X, "in which either from an excessive devotion to the Venetian materialistic manner, or his own tendency to Nature gaining too great an ascendancy over his idealistic powers," Raphael was satisfied by mere "illusory transcription of physical forms" (*ASE*, 283). The passage is interesting among other things for what appears in a subsequent sentence Wallace's only—and not too complimentary—reference to Rembrandt: "There is, one might almost say, a cannibalism of materiality which goes below Rembrandt." Furthermore, the passage leads to the statement of an important aesthetic principle: "Art does not consist in representing forms; it consists in causing forms to represent thoughts, sentiments, emotions" (*ASE*, 284). The fragmentary nature of this essay, with its abrupt interruptions and jottings, suggests, especially in light of the varied allusions through the series, that Wallace intended not only to put his thoughts on Raphael into final form but probably to write on other painters as well.

III *Travel Notes*

Wallace's "Notes of a Tour of Switzerland" takes a closer and more contemplative look at Alpine scenery than does the average travel book of the time. In his almost religious reverence for nature, Wallace seems to have come a few steps closer to the Transcendentalists since his previous writings. "Our native and familiar earth," he writes of the Alps, "is seen expanding into the sublimity of the heavens, and we feel as if our destiny were exalted along with it." As he admires Michelangelo's art for its power in repose, so he finds consolation in "the quietness of power . . . in which these mighty eminences rest, living out their great lives in silent and motionless serenity" (*ASE*, 135). Everywhere he exhibits a high degree of pictorial sensitivity. He is interested in vantage point, contrast, color. He likes "a great distant view," for "great mountains are like great men; the true picturesque point of view is a remote one" (*ASE*, 136). Watching the Jungfrau from the Wengern Alp, he notes the difference between "the pearly white of the foaming clouds" and "the metallic radiance of the icy mountains" against the blue sky (*ASE*, 140). From the top of the Fauldhorn he sees no longer individual mountains but "one great broad wall of

snow-covered rock . . . the stupendous barrier that nature has set
between the North and South of Europe." Then he turns to the
sunset, recording every change in color and resultant feeling, struck
at last by "the very slight effect which so considerable an oc-
currence, as the setting of the sun, had upon these great objects,
while the inferior realm had been in a tumult of agitation" (ASE,
144 - 47).

Wallace pauses from time to time in his meticulous and evoca-
tive observations of nature to make a literary or historical allusion.
He speaks of Byron more than once, and he devotes several pages
to the Castle of Chillon. He pays tribute to Bonnivard, its famous
sixteenth-century prisoner, before whose courage "the sentimental
fancy of Byron's tale fades into insignificance" (ASE, 168)—
something that Byron himself had acknowledged. We seem to hear
an echo of the young Wallace, author of Henry Pulteney, as
we read the grim account of the Hall of Justice, "so called from the
injustices judicially performed there," the torture room, the
oubliette, the prison and execution rooms underground. "Two
thousand Jews were reported to have been hanged or strangled
here, upon a charge of poisoning the fountains, but really for the
purpose of confiscating their wealth. Opposite the gallows, hung
formerly a picture of the Virgin, on which the dying man might
look." And Wallace adds the finely ironic point: "A solace that
must have been particularly welcome to the Jews" (ASE, 170).

Unlike other travel accounts, the "Notes" contains little personal
element and almost no anecdotal material. Wallace uses the first
person singular freely and makes a more or less exact record of his
movements, but we can only surmise that his occasional "we" includes only himself and his guide, rather than his brother or
someone else with whom he might have been traveling. The "I" of
the account freely records observations and feelings, but they
might be anyone's; there seems to be a scrupulous avoidance of
biographical material outside the journey. All the more welcome
are occasional personal touches such as being served dinner at a
certain inn "by one of the handsomest women that I have seen in
Switzerland. Her dignified, mild features, set off by the peculiar
gilded turban of the Vallais, which resembles a coronet, might have
graced the proudest court in Europe." On going to bed that night,
"I fell asleep, with the murmurs of the infant Rhone in my ears,
and visions of crowned Madonnas in my fancy" (ASE, 154).

How much Wallace was the writer, who traveled and observed

and felt and thought with pencil in hand, becomes evident from those random pieces—in the form of reports or letters—which he produced everywhere he went. We have touched on two of these, "Visit to Netley Abbey" and "Ascent of Vesuvius," biographically. There are a few additonal ones that have come down. "Letter from Florence" to the *Home Journal*[14] reports on the work of such American sculptors living abroad as Crawford, Powers, and Greenough. A second "Letter from Florence" to the *Home Journal*[15] speaks of the sights, with special emphasis on the Cathedral. In "The Roman Forum" Wallace muses over "Rome of the mind," specifically, Rome's great legal heritage and her ultimate role as a vehicle of Christianity (*ASE*, 187 - 89). "Letter from Paris" to the *Home Journal*[16] regrets the presence of too many Americans, who tend to be interested only in the frivolities Paris has to offer. A second letter from Paris, written to William B. Wood, actor and manager of the Chestnut Street Theater in Philadelphia, to whom Wallace subsequently left a hundred dollars, touches on a variety of experiences abroad, including performances of Shakespeare and Racine, as well as "morbid musings, which are oppressive, and yet fascinating," upon the Coliseum, that "emblem of the inevitable ruin of all national greatness." We get here a statement of Wallace's final unqualified admiration for Byron and a glimpse of "beautiful girls" in Italy, "with flashing dark eyes promising mystery." Throughout there is a welcome personal note. Wallace is bringing a chip of stone from Juliet's tomb for a breastpin for Wood's daughter, and in a playful tone he refers to the Woods and himself rehearsing the Siege of Dendermond at the bottom of the garden. Like his account of his visit to Comte, this letter owes its survival to posthumous publication in the *Home Journal*.[17]

CHAPTER 6

Positivism

I   *Wallace and Auguste Comte*

THE word "philosophy" in the title of the first post-humous collection of Wallace's works denotes a fifteen-page reprint from the *Methodist Quarterly Review*,[1] in which Wallace expressed his view of Comte's philosophy in the last year of his life. Since this essay is in some important respects critical, whereas Comte saw in Wallace his most important American disciple, it is necessary that the Wallace-Comte relationship be traced here in some detail.

In the development of human reason, says Comte in the *first phase* of his philosophy, there occur three stages, or states, of explaining phenomena: the theological, seeking supernatural causes; the metaphysical, seeking abstract causes; and the positive, seeking natural laws. Interrelated with these three states, the sciences have followed an order of development which tends toward increasing specialization and closeness to man, our understanding of each science depending on all the preceding ones. This order is mathematics, astronomy, physics, chemistry, biology, reaching an apex in the most recent science of Comte's own recognition and designation, sociology. The ultimate aim of the positive method, according to Comte, is to establish a Religion of Humanity, which he develops in the *second phase* of his philosophy. It is a system complete with sainted heroes of human progress, rituals, and with Comte himself reigning as high priest.

The first phase of positivism—the law of the three states and the hierarchy of the sciences—was set down by Comte in his *Cours de philosophie positive* (1830 - 42) in six large volumes of often heavy-handed and verbose French, which Wallace had studied before paying his first visit to Comte in the spring of 1851. One recalls that the upshot of this visit was Wallace's promise of a five hundred-franc annuity to the philosopher. Comte wrote to several of his disciples about the "very interesting visit of an eminent Philadelphian," who had told him of the recent emergence of a "positivist center [*foyer positivist*]" both in Philadelphia and in New York.[2] In one of these letters Comte speaks of positivism being appreciated in America not only as pure philosophy but also as the one social guarantee against communism.[3]

That this is an exaggerated account of the interest in positivism in America at this time is clear from such a study as Richmond L. Hawkins's *Auguste Comte and the United States (1816 - 1853)*.[4] The question here is whether the exaggeration was more Wallace's account or Comte's interpretation. Comte, it is generally known, took an almost fanatical interest in the spread of his doctrine; at the same time, Wallace's first letter to him from America suggests that during his visit in April he himself may have given an overenthusiastic account of both his own and others' reception of Comte's *Cours de philosophie positive*. His letter of June 23, 1851, reaffirms his offer of the annuity, stating, "In establishing the law of the three methods of philosophising—and the law of the hierarchy of the sciences—I think You have made more valuable contributions to the truth than anyone in this age. I desire to recognize the obligation that is due You, though it is not in my power to discharge it." Wallace continues: "I shall take an early opportunity to express some opinions to You upon the subject of the application of the Positive Philosophy to the present crisis in France." Finally he asks Comte to elaborate on "some of the topics which formed the subjects of our conversations—especially the religious aspects of the new philosophy."[5]

For this was the time of Comte's working out the second, or religious, phase of his system, the first volume of his *Système de politique positive* about to appear just that year. Comte's answer to Wallace is now lost; but in a letter to one of his disciples, Dr. Georges Audiffrent, Comte mentions having replied to Wallace the next day at length, commenting on "the true guardian angels and the institution of our new social sacraments," and formally authorizing Mr. Wallace to divulge the contents of his letter to such as he sees fit. In the same letter to Audiffrent, Comte speaks of the five hundred francs as the "least equivocal symptom, among the rich, of true positivist convictions."[6]

Wallace waited seven months to reply to Comte, writing to him on March 4, 1852: "Your charming letter of last summer, which I have repeatedly read, has given me many most valuable Suggestions; & in accordance with your indication, I have shown it to such persons as appeared to be likely to understand and profit of it." After apologizing for his tardy reply, he adds: "Nevertheless, as I know that the communication of knowledge to those who are disposed to appreciate it, is to You a sufficient reward in itself, I venture to assure You that by none will Your instructions be more valued than by myself. If, in advance of the publication of your books, there are any discoveries which you are in the habit of making known by lectures or conversations, to those who have the privilege to approach You, your friends on this side of the Atlantic, would welcome the communication of such matters by letter." Wallace notes further: "The first volume of your 'Système de Politique Positive' was received here last autumn & I am told by the booksellers, that many copies have been sold."[7]

II "Comte's Philosophy"

If there is the faintest suggestion in this letter that Wallace was somewhat reserved toward the ritualistic aspects of Comte's Religion of Humanity, that he perhaps showed Comte's letter to fewer people than Comte might have preferred, in short, that he was not the devout disciple Comte took him to be, the public letter Wallace was composing just about this time would bear such a suggestion out. In January, 1852, there had appeared in the *Methodist Quarterly Review* the first part of George F. Holmes's article, "Faith and Science—Comte's Positive Philosophy."[8] It was in effect a review of *Cours de philosophie positive* ten years after its appearance. Wallace, feeling that Holmes had misunderstood certain ideas of Comte, set to work on an article of his own in the form of a letter to the editor, the Rev. John M'Clintock, whom Wallace knew personally. This letter appeared a year after Wallace's death in the *Methodist Quarterly Review*, and was then reprinted in *Art, Scenery and Philosophy in Europe* as "Comte's Philosophy."[9]

The letter falls naturally into two portions: Wallace's acceptance of what he believes to be the most important of Comte's doctrines; secondly, his rejection of Comte's atheistic implications together with his Religion of Humanity. The "most important truth which M. Comte has conceived,—the very *core* of truth of the system of

Positive Philosophy" Wallace believes to be the hierarchy of the sciences. For, Wallace explains, it is wrong to think, as Descartes thought, that science deals only with the "external and material" and not with the "mental." Comte has extended the scope of science, which both he and Bacon conceive as "a knowledge of the laws of the relation or reaction of things." But it must be remembered that the sciences are essentially different from each other. Mathematics, "which is not, as is popularly imagined, in the nature of a 'philosophia prima,' or 'scientia scientiarum,'" deals with the magnitude of physical things. On a higher level there is chemistry, which studies reactions where "the axioms of mathematics no longer apply," where "the whole is not equal to all its parts any longer." It is interesting to note in the present context this almost exact restatement of an earlier observation in *Stanley*, which Poe later copied into his "Purloined Letter." "As we go up in the scale of sciences," Wallace continues, "the conceptive part, or that which is occupied in establishing the primary laws, becomes larger and more laborious, and the logical part smaller. Chemistry . . . never can be (to man's intellect) capable of the simplicity and generality of mathematical conception, nor the rigour and exactitude of mathematical reasoning." Next, there are the biological sciences, "yet more concrete, special, indeterminate, and variable than chemistry." In the last stage, "we arrive at political relations, with the various branches of intellectual, moral, and spiritual." That there are laws in this area, says Wallace, was first suggested not by Comte but by King David and the Old Testament prophets. These laws are God's, but science may investigate them, for "there is positive *science* of moral and political truth." However, "scientific conceptions, as applied to social subjects, will, perhaps, hardly ever get beyond some very general notion of the character of laws. . . . M. Comte, I apprehend, never uttered so monstrous a fallacy and sciolism, as that *mathematical* science is applicable to social subjects" (*ASPE*, 338).

But fortunately, says Wallace, what we lose in certainty as we ascend higher among the sciences, we gain in applicability. "In regard to politics, the establishment . . . of the mere *fact* that the subject is governed by inherent laws, though no one of those laws should ever be discovered, or even remotely indicated, would be the greatest benefit ever conferred upon the world of a temporal kind: because at once it would enable us to repel and destroy the

assaults of all those metaphysical sophisms—as that all men have
equal rights—all political power rightfully springs only from the
consent of the governed—which have tormented and vexed society
like diseases" (*ASPE*, 339).

Is such anti-democratic dogma the ultimate aim of Wallace's
own brand of positivism? Of special interest is his pejorative use of
"metaphysical," which half a page later he is all too eager to accept
again as a legitimate mode of inquiry, as he attempts to clarify the
three states of explaining phenomena: "I do not understand that
M. Comte explodes, as destitute of truth, the theological and
metaphysical methods or forms of philosophy. They are just and
true, according to their own point of view; but they contemplate
different purposes from the positive. . . . I see no reason why, in
their complete development, they should not all exist together"
(*ASPE*, 340).

Wallace is now ready to dissent from Comte's atheism, which
"may be the accident of the individual" but "not a characteristic of
the system." Since positivism is "a certain and universal method"
and religion is "a reality as certain as life itself . . . the correct
application of the positive method to the subject of religion, so far
from upsetting, will verify and demonstrate the catholic faith. In
attempting this application M. Comte has altogether broken down"
(*ASPE*, 341).

What Wallace means by "catholic faith" will appear later. He
continues: "I think that I can state to you precisely the character
and extent of M. Comte's intellectual merit, and draw the line
within which he is an oracle and beyond which he is a babbler."
For, like Bacon, Comte shines in "abstract and logical reasoning"
but fails in "practical sagacity in investigation." As the *Cours de
philosophie positive* shows his "prodigious powers" in the former,
so the *Système de politique positive*—of which Wallace had seen at
this time only the first volume—shows his "puny capacity" in the
latter. Wallace similarly takes to task Émil Littré, an important disciple of Comte, whose liberal politics, however, were to prove in-
compatible with the master's conservative ones. "M. Comte thinks
that Positivism is Atheistic. M. Littré thinks that it is republican or
radical. I agree with neither. I am a conservative of the conser-
vatives: and it is upon the positive system, as applied to morals and
politics, that I found my confidence in the ultimate triumph of
sound principles" (*ASPE*, 341 - 43).

Nor is Comte the discoverer of the positive method. "A student
of Bacon and of those great men who after him had taken up and

extended the inductive method, I was myself engaged in applying it to politics, morals, and spirituality, before I heard of Comte." Wallace goes on to say that he has long endeavored to rectify Comte's aberrations in these areas and he promises a contribution of "some slight suggestions" of his own to positivism insofar as it is destined to demonstrate the revealed truth of Christianity and thereby "convert the world."

Similarly in the area of politics, he sees positivism as the only safeguard against "the disorganizing maxims and passions of the revolutionary and destructive parties of the day"—a statement that provides a clue as to the source of Comte's belief that Americans looked to positivism as a social guarantee against communism. Wallace speaks of having been occupied for some time with a history of political philosophy, which he would "perhaps complete in the form of a report to the Smithsonian Institute. I desire therein to trace the rise, and operation, and failure of all the metaphysical systems, and the rise, and partial developments, and imperfect apprehension of it [sic] down to the present day" (*ASPE*, 344).

Wallace concludes by expressing a distaste for the introduction of positivism in its present incomplete state to the public. He thinks that the article by Holmes that he is answering "will do no harm, for nobody will understand what it is all about." But he does not care to see positivism in the hands of "the mob of litterateurs in this country. . . . Let the people stand out of the way, until the positive development of morals and politics is complete; and then let it be brought before them, not as a thing to speculate about, or dogmatize about—but to receive, and to submit to as they do to the teachings of the mathematician and the chemist. Besides this, until the positive scheme can be shown as a scheme tending to and ending in religion, identical with revealed religion, the public knowledge of it will only tend to evil" (*ASPE*, 345).

In his *Auguste Comte and the United States*, R. L. Hawkins devotes considerable space to this letter by Wallace, largely to show that Wallace was a disciple of Comte to a far lesser extent than Comte believed and claimed. The letter has the additional importance of being, if not a final statement of Wallace's intellectual development, the final indication of the direction it would have taken. Wallace's assertion, for example, that Comte's teachings will act on the world only *mediately* Hawkins calls "prophetic, since most of the philosophers and savants of the second half of the nineteenth century were influenced by Comte" (p. 74). This is an important point, for between the handful of true disciples, such as

Henry Edger, who went along with Comte all the way, and Comte's highly sceptical critics among the American clergy, Wallace was able to steer a clear enough course. He saw the importance and the greater and greater ascendancy of the scientific method; and saw perhaps even more importantly, in the first part of his essay, that the scientific method could not, however, be applied in the social and ethical realm with as much exactitude as in the physical or even biological sciences.

But must the compatibility of positivism and religion be necessarily resolved in the fantastic notion of "demonstrating" the veracity of revealed religion by the positive method? How would Wallace have proceeded in this? His own tentative answer to this question involving a new form of Christian faith, which we shall presently come to, is hardly sufficient. The more carefully the letter is read, the more clearly there emerges, especially through the latter part, a certain emotional exaggeration—almost a loss at times of control.

We have already noted Wallace's equivocal use of "metaphysical" and his loose interpretation of Comte's religious innovation. Wallace seems to clutch the cross here as in no previous work, and his political stance—his desperate denial of "the democratic maxims of the rights of man" seems no longer a mere expression of conservatism but an attack on the American system itself, which in previous writings he always defended. There is little reason to doubt either his personal respect or his friendly feelings, even affection, toward Comte evidenced in his letters to him; critical objectivity does not quite account for the sharp contrast here of such apellatives as "oracle" and "babbler." We hear the voice of a kind of Christian hero trying to wrest the "good" Comte from the "enemy" Comte. Wallace reveals his ambition here as nowhere else. The aim is "to convert the world"—a concept reminiscent of the aim of the fictional Tyler—a kind of atheistic positivist—to conquer the world by the means of unscrupulous practical intelligence. Only in his attempt to divide Comte, Wallace himself was being divided. Throughout the letter the ominous signs point the way to the crisis later on that year when the cross would be of little aid.

That Wallace himself saw something of these feverish exaggerations is suggested by the fact that he refrained from sending his letter to M'Clintock. Presumably he wanted to see it published, wanted to answer Holmes, probably under his own name; for his association with Comte was becoming known—but only aftec he had made revisions. He apparently never did. When M'Clintock published Wallace's letter in his *Methodist Quarterly Review*, he eliminated the last paragraph, which is such a fervent plea for censorship. More important, he prefaced the piece with the adjective "unfinished," clarifying it in the next sentence: "The reader will understand that it had no revision from the author's hand."

III   *Comte and Others on Wallace*

More tempered, while in essential accord, is a personal letter Wallace wrote several months later to another student of Comte, the Reverend Joseph Henry Allen of Bangor, Maine. Having seen Wallace mentioned in the Preface to the second volume of Comte's *Système de politique positive* as "the eminent Philadelphian, who has become my principal temporal patron without ceasing to be my noble spiritual client,"[10] Allen wrote to Wallace, presumably to seek further information about positivists in America. Wallace's reply on September 11, 1852, begins negatively, almost coldly, claiming less knowledge about those interested in Comte than he could perhaps have mustered. He says he views with regret the formation of a Positivist Society in France and is against the formation of any such society in America, which would tend to propagate "the founder's personal system of opinions" with its "many defects & errors." Wallace reasserts the rightness of the positive method, which like astronomy or chemistry needs no "cabal of persons to sustain or enforce it." Although Comte is in no sense the founder of the positive method, he has made more contributions to it than anyone since Bacon. "The world is under unmeasurable obligations to him," and he deserves "personal support." Wallace's tone remains temperate as he points to Comte's "synthetic" attempts to reconstruct society and the "metaphysical fabric of error" he has woven around the subject of religion. Contrarily, Wallace is confident that "the positive method can be brought to bear upon religion with perfect success." Concluding on a warmer note, Wallace suggests that Allen visit him if ever in Philadelphia.[11]

Allen did, on November 5, asking Wallace to elucidate the application of the positive method to religion. "In reply," Allen wrote to Griswold early in 1853, after Wallace's death," he said, in general terms, that he thought this method would result in a religious system bearing more analogies to the Catholic than any other existing one: only (if I understood him rightly) resting on the development of the free reason, and on the entire historical development of mankind, instead of ecclesiastic dogmatism, and a practical view of history."[12]

His sharp divergence from Comte's later thought did not prevent Wallace from visiting Comte three days before his death and giving him five hundred francs for the coming year. His manner during this visit was no doubt respectful and kindly, although he did not remain entirely silent on the subject of religion, speaking, in Comte's words, of "a separation . . . between religion and irreligion, between the creators and the destroyers."[13] Comte, who later referred to this visit as "sacred," noting "the sad tone" of Wallace's farewell,[14] summed up his thoughts about Wallace in the Preface to the third volume of his *Système de politique positive*, which appeared in the summer of 1853. He speaks here of the "exceptional catastrophe which deprived me recently of an eminent disciple destined to become one of the pillars of positivism," who "would have been bound to make an important contribution to the difficult transition awaiting the nineteenth century" (p. xvii). Comte's four-paragraph eulogy reaches its culmination in an "intellectual and moral" comparison between Wallace and Jefferson—something that Wallace would have scarcely appreciated and his brother pointedly deleted when quoting Comte's tribute in the "Memoir" and in the front matter of the two posthumous collections.

Comte continued to write about Wallace both in his correspondence and in his published works, until his own death in 1857, expressing his gratitude more than once for the annuity which Wallace had willed to him for life. In his "Ninth St. Clotilde," for 1853, one of the yearly confessions he wrote and read at the tomb of his great love, Clotilde de Vaux, he mentions Wallace as one of his brothers within his "subjective family."[15] In his *Synthèse subjective* (1856) Comte reproduced Wallace's first letter to him after his visit of 1851, prefacing it with his usual tribute to Wallace's memory. In his concluding remarks he makes the curious assertion that during his final visit, three days before his death, Wallace "expressed to me, in a most touching manner, his complete adherence upon his recent study of the first two volumes of my religious construction. His great soul had appreciated deeply the noble social activity which positivism is substituting for those insufficient personal satisfactions which were naturally appropriate to theology" (p. xxv).

That Wallace was less than completely candid about his opinion of Comte's religious views during that last visit has already been suggested. But that he was guilty of complete insincerity is harder to believe than that Comte is here projecting his need for Wallace's complete "adherence." Students of Comte have noted this tendency in him; here there is a similar indication. At any rate, it does not appear that Comte ever saw—or perhaps that he even wanted to see—Wallace's sharp, almost insulting comments about his "religious construction," which by September, 1855, when he wrote the above Preface, were out in two versions. John M'Clintock, who corresponded with Comte, might well have refrained from sending him the January, 1854, issue of the *Methodist Quarterly Review* containing Wallace's letter. But there is little doubt that John Wallace, who had written to Comte about a forthcoming collection of his brother's writings,[16] presented him with a copy of *Art, Scenery and Philosophy in Europe*.[17] Possibly, Comte's English was sufficiently weak to provide a natural barrier.[18] At any rate, as late as February, 1857, in writing to Henry Edger about John Wallace's possible embracing of "our faith," Comte referred to him as "the worthy brother of my late eminent disciple."[19]

More realistic seems to have been Comte's truer disciple, Henry Edger's view of Wallace's "conversion." In 1856 Edger published his *Positivist Calendar* at the progressive community, Modern Times (later Brentwood), Long Island, with a full-page dedication to the Memory of Wallace.[20] In the Preface, Edger quotes the last two pages of Wallace's "Comte's Philosophy," giving the admittedly misleading editorial comment at the end, "MS. unfinished," a literal interpretation by saying,

At this point the MS. was abruptly terminated by the writer's untimely death. Had he happily lived long enough to become acquainted with the real nature and characteristics of the Grand Religious Construction of M. Comte, he could not have failed to have modified the estimate formed of it previous to its complete development, seeing that it realizes all his organic social tendencies in a higher degree than even he himself contemplated, while, on the other hand, it equally satisfies the noble and generous aspirations of the progressive parties on behalf of freedom and popular well-being, aspirations which the position and social antecedents of Wallace prevented his estimating at their true value. (p. x)

If this is double-talk, one way out of it is to return to Wallace, who argued that positivism can be applied to various ends. But the perhaps excessively optimistic Edger does make the effort in this passage to grapple with Wallace's deep-seated conservatism; and he puts the matter right in the concluding passage which pays tribute to Wallace as "one of the most energetic coöperators in the one great understanding which constitutes the sole necessary initiative and principal permanent basis of the Positivist movement" (p. x). He means of course the law of the three states and the hierarchy of the sciences, laid down in the six volumes of the *Cours de philosophie positive*. It is here that Comte developed the science of sociology, on which his greatest fame rests today. In a broader sense, then, however contrarily to Comte's narrower expectations, Wallace can be said to have played an important role at the source of the intellectual movement without which the modern world would be inconceivable.

CHAPTER 7

Fame Against the Odds

I Posthumous Collections

I T would appear that at the time of his death Wallace was preparing the thoughts and observations resulting from his European trip of 1850 - 51 for book publication. At one point Griswold seems to have felt sufficiently encouraged to draft an agreement between "the Author of 'Art and Scenery in Europe' " and J. S. Redfield, who was publishing his four-volume edition of Poe.[1] But Wallace probably wanted more time for revision. According to the "Memoir," the material was with him in Paris when he died. Stressing that "the papers which follow . . . *are all unfinished,*"[2] John Wallace probably supplied the few editorial comments needed and gave the manuscript to a friend of the Wallaces, the Reverend Herman Hooker, who ran a publishing house in Philadelphia. Hooker himself may have had a hand in some aspect of the editing, possibly in the arrangement of the material. Writing to Griswold some time in 1854 to ask him for publicity, he notes, "The volume is to include what the author designed for a volume"; and he justifies an edition of only one thousand copies by saying, "Wallace was not known—and there are pretenders enough who will not wish to see his light: Let us hail it Milton-like, as a first burst of creation."[3]

In November the book was out, bearing the title: *Art, Scenery and Philosophy in Europe. Being the Fragments from the Port-Folio of the late Horace Binney Wallace, Esquire, of Philadelphia.* The prefatory matter included commendations of Wallace by Daniel Webster and Comte, the "Memoir," and Horace Binney's "Obituary." The substance of the volume was the material discussed in the two previous chapters.

The mask was off. Julia Ward Howe wrote,

139

> They bring a volume, precious with thy name
> And latest records—all that Love can save,
> While the snow falls upon the two-years' grave
> Where thy dear ashes careless lie of fame. . . .[4]

John Wallace and his late brother's friends nevertheless commenced to construct a belated literary fame. It was a difficult task on two accounts. During his lifetime Wallace had worked so persistently against fame that there was now little to anchor the volume to. The Danas knew Wallace well, yet one of them was "astonished Wallace could write so beautiful a book and worthy of study."[5] Secondly, as the prudent limitation of the edition to one thousand copies indicates, the book was caviar to the general. "Isn't it a dinner for one hungry in Art," wrote Charles Godfrey Leland to Griswold;[6] but there were relatively few Americans hungry for art in the middle of the nineteenth century.

Yet the efforts largely of John Wallace and Herman Hooker, and possibly Griswold, in placing copies began to pay off in a proliferation of reviews.[7] The *New Englander*[8] devoted over four pages to the book. Although the reviewer disagrees with Wallace's judgment that the Reformation dealt a serious blow to art, he speaks with admiration of Wallace's "high intellectual character . . . his natural superiority, and extraordinary attainments." Two months later, in July, 1855, the *North American Review* published Sidney George Fisher's thirty-page review.[9] Its greater portion develops the reviewer's own views on such themes as great men, history, and beauty, but there remains much space to quote from Wallace. Fisher says at one point that in calling art symbolical rather than imitative, Wallace "attributes too much to the imagination of the artist, and too little to the expressive power of nature" (p. 229)—an objection hardly convincing to the modern reader—but essentially he hails Wallace's book.

George W. Curtis rated *Art, Scenery and Philosophy in Europe* "among the most remarkable and valuable in American aesthetic literature."[10] Parke Godwin shows a degree of psychological insight as well, saying that Wallace's excessive modesty caused him to make "fewer public trials of his powers than their unquestionable superiority would have warranted." But he feels that the present book is "a rich repayment of Wallace's reticence."[11] His chief objection is to Wallace's sharp isolation of the visual arts from music

and literature, which are all "necessary to each other, because
necessary to the complete expression of man's artistic capacity" (p.
320). The disagreement seems here to be merely a question of
emphasis; Godwin seems to be on more solid ground in his objection that Wallace's association of artistic inspiration with religious
belief is somewhat narrow.

No literary friend could have done more to keep Wallace's name
before the public than George P. Morris. From March to August,
1855, the *Home Journal* published no less than nine substantial articles dealing with Wallace—notices of his book, excerpts from it,
letters by him during his European travels, excerpts from reviews
appearing in other periodicals.[12]

Meanwhile John Wallace was preparing the second posthumous
collection. The idea for this volume had originated in his mind
probably soon after his brother's death. Herman Hooker writing to
Griswold on April 29, 1853, mentions a scrapbook John Wallace has
shown him of his brother's "pieces and reviews in the newspapers
for the last ten years, with his letters from Europe. . . . He is considering publishing them."[13] Since putting this volume together
required more editorial work than did the previous one, as well as
an awareness of some of the intricacies of the American literary
scene, it is possible that John Wallace relegated much of the task,
perhaps all of it, to someone else. Herman Hooker remains a
possibility, although the publisher was this time Parry and McMillan.
The book appeared early in 1856, bearing the title: *Literary
Criticisms and Other Papers. By the Late Horace Binney Wallace,
Esquire, of Philadelphia.* The volume is dedicated to George P.
Morris by the editor, and among the testimonials there appear
tributes once again by Webster and Comte. But the prefatory
matter is confined to two pages, briefly introducing Wallace, his
works, and the contents of the present volume. These are mostly
reprints of literary articles and reviews examined in previous
chapters; a good portion of the book consists of the literary
dialogues Wallace had incorporated into *Stanley* and *Henry
Pulteney*, but, as has been noted, without any editorial reference to
those novels.[14]

Once again Morris did his utmost for the book. Immediately
before and for several months after its appearance, the *Home Journal* published many long columns of excerpts, together with other
Wallace material such as some of Wallace's correspondence with

"Fanny Forester."[15] On May 17, 1856, the *Home Journal* spoke of the generally favorable reception of *Literary Criticisms;* less than a week later, John Wallace wrote to the elder Dana,

> Both of my brother's books are just now exhausted here: though pretty good editions of both were printed. The Art Scenery &c. was not stereotyped. There will be a second edn. of both.
>
> The last one was intended by me rather as a supplemental volume . . . in showing another side of his mind, & a full view of his *heart.* There must be some, who have not liked its political opinions & some who have not liked its religious notions. Still it has been highly eulogized & no where more than in the last Number of The *Democratic* Review, which surprises me; and 1000 copies were sold at once. A new edition is now ordered. I meant to bring out . . . a volume of correspondence which would have explained the circumstances under which many of these pieces were written . . . so as to have relieved the work from an imputation, which has been made in one instance, of an insensibility to *"relative"* literary merit. Many of the pieces were written as replies to very unjust attacks.[16]

The *Democratic Review* certainly gave *Literary Criticisms* high praise, which, coming from Wallace's political opponents, is all the more noteworthy. The reviewer speaks of "real criticism," which "you may hear if you will listen a little to Mr. Wallace. . . . Where friendship does not bind its bandage over his eyes, he sees with a free and learned spirit into the heart of things. He has an artist's eye, and a poet's instinct, combined with the ripe judgment and polished keenness of a critic." Although his style is "rather elaborate, and not always transparent," his writing has the merit of "frequent novelty, as well as profound philosophy." He dares to think for himself and "that strange spell, a name, has no power to paralyze him. . . . With little slips induced by personal friendship taken away, he stands foremost, to our mind, amongst American critics."[17]

But the great surprise and enthusiasm with which the previous volume had been received seems to have spent itself. Reviews devoted specifically to *Literary Criticisms* are hard to find. In July, 1856, there appeared in the *Knickerbocker Magazine*[18] a four-page article speaking of both posthumous volumes, but it tends to be more of an obituary than a review. Interestingly, it deems Wallace's writings, however energetic and luminous, mechanical in comparison with "the charm and frequently amazing power of his modestly and quietly-delivered discourse."

For the second edition of *Art, Scenery and Philosophy in Europe,* John Wallace chose the title that his brother had originally conceived for the work: *Art and Scenery in Europe,* adding: *With Other Papers: Being Chiefly Fragments from the Port-Folio of the Late Horace Binney Wallace, Esquire, of Philadelphia.* This volume appeared at the end of 1856, bearing the date 1857. The publishers were again Parry and McMillan, who made the book a companion piece to the previous *Literary Criticisms* in format. *Art and Scenery in Europe* is substantially different from its similarly-titled predecessor. The prefatory matter is cut to a minimum and "Comte's Philosophy" is replaced by some one hundred and seventy-five pages of editorial articles and other journalistic pieces that appeared mainly in the *Home Journal* and an excerpt from Wallace's essay on Washington.

George P. Morris once again came to the fore in the columns of the *Home Journal,* but there were few new notices, as might be expected. On November, 1856, the *Home Journal* spoke of the edition which had just come off the press as already exhausted, but a subsequent edition of *Art and Scenery in Europe* does not appear to have been published until twelve years later.[19] On November 29, the *Home Journal* expressed the hope that Wallace's correspondence might be given to the world, but, ironically, little besides the handful of letters which in fact the *Home Journal* printed posthumously has survived. Here we might ask also of the identity and the fate of those sixteen volumes which the "Memoir" mentions as the extent of Wallace's literary output. They seem to be alluded to in John Wallace's letter to the elder Dana on August 30, 1855: "You rightly conjectured that I have in view, *at some time,* to bring out a collection of his writings, in some handsome form: but when this will be I cannot say."[20] We know nothing further. What we have today of Wallace's non-legal writings represents but a small portion of any such bulk.

II *Surviving Reputation*

Wallace's literary achievement was given its first relatively permanent recognition by the Duyckinck brothers' influential *Cyclopaedia of American Literature,* which appeared in 1855. Here a biographical article and an excerpt from his essay on St. Peter's running to two columns placed Wallace in a respectable position with reference to other American writers—something that Griswold

had tried so hard to achieve during Wallace's lifetime, un-
successfully. A similar work of less literary but greater scholarly
scope, Samuel A. Allibone's *Critical Dictionary of English
Literature* (1858 - 71) devoted over a column to Wallace, with am-
ple bibliographical references. All important general and
biographical encyclopedias of the period gave Wallace due space.
Parke Godwin, in reprinting his review of *Art, Scenery and
Philosophy in Europe* in his collection, *Out of the Past*, in 1870,
clearly thought of Wallace as a noted literary figure.

A marked decline in Wallace's reputation occurred during the
decades following the Civil War. A reasonable explanation would
be that this was a period characterized by realism and political
progressivism—a period dominated by Mark Twain, the regional-
ists, and the democratic voice of Walt Whitman. Not that aesthetic
sensibility was entirely dead. The great original impulse of a Poe
pushed on, and there was Henry James, and side by side with
Naturalism at the end of the century there was also a revived concern with beauty, as in the poetic side of Stephen Crane—to name
only one, the perhaps most intriguing, example. But Wallace's
quiet, refined, conservative, and essentially minor voice could not
be heard. By the end of the century the connection between
Wallace and "William Landor" was broken, a copy of *Stanley* was
a rarity, while Wallace's posthumous collections lodged unread and
unknown in our major libraries.

An interesting but sadly abortive attempt to re-establish
Wallace's reputation was made in the beginning of the twentieth
century by Clarence E. Ward, a Boston lawyer and editor of a thin
volume of selections from Shakespeare. In 1908, Ward, a great admirer of Wallace, wrote to Princeton for information about him,
saying that he was writing a "literary memoir" of him which he expected Houghton-Mifflin to publish.[21] Ward completed the
manuscript and sent it to Houghton-Mifflin, where it lay for some
time unpublished. After Ward's death the manuscript was returned
to Ward's son, an officer in the Marine Corps, who destroyed it.[22]

It is thanks to the literary scholars of the present century that
Wallace has not been entirely forgotten. Robert E. Spiller's article
on Wallace in the *Dictionary of American Biography*, that important descendent of nineteenth-century encyclopedias, is a major
modern source. Willard Thorp in the *Literary History of the
United States*[23] and Van Wyck Brooks in his *Times of Melville and
Whitman*[24] mention Wallace only briefly; but R. L. Hawkins's

work on the influence of Comte in America and Joy Bayless's work on Griswold led both of these scholars to a somewhat detailed treatment of Wallace in their books. In 1956, there appeared John P. Pritchard's *Criticism in America*,[25] which makes a number of references to Wallace. Finally in 1972 there occurred the important event in Wallace scholarship of the reprinting of *Literary Criticisms* by the Books for Libraries Press. Altogether the signs are favorable for Wallace to gain the place he shunned but deserves in our literature.

Notes and References

The following abbreviations are used in this section and, in some cases, in the text:

NP - National Press
HJ - Home Journal
ASPE - Art, Scenery and Philosophy in Europe
ASE - Art and Scenery in Europe with Other Papers
LC - Literary Criticisms and Other Papers

Preface

1. *New Yorker*, 6 (Dec. 22, 1838), 221.
2. Freeport, N.Y.: Books for Libraries Press, 1972.
3. John W. Wallace's authorship of the "Memoir" is nowhere explicitly stated; but since his correspondence with R. H. Dana, Sr. (at the Massachusetts Historical Society) shows him to be the moving spirit of the posthumous publications, and the "Memoir" reveals a family member's intimate acquaintance with its subject and quotes from family letters, his authorship can be safely assumed. The Library of Congress Catalogue attributes the "Memoir," as well as the following "Obituary," to Horace Binney. This is clearly an error, since the "Memoir" quotes a passage from the "Obituary," attributing it to "the highest legal authority at the bar in this country" (p. xiv). Binney's "Obituary" first appeared as a pamphlet (Philadelphia: C. Sherman, 1853).
4. In the first two editions of the Duyckinck brothers' *Cyclopaedia of American Literature* (New York: Scribner, 1855 and 1856). On October 13, 1857, George P. Morris communicated to Evert A. Duyckinck John W. Wallace's desire to have the word "suicide" excised from future editions. (Ms. letter, New York Public Library.) The Duyckincks complied, but the fact was out.
5. "Memoir," *ASPE*, p. xvi; Ms. letter to R. H. Dana, Sr., Aug. 30, 1855, Massachusetts Historical Society.
6. That John Wallace was not averse to destroying personal or literary papers is shown by his letter to R. H. Dana, Sr. on October 30, 1862 (Massachusetts Historical Society), in which he speaks of Rufus W. Griswold's having appointed him and George H. Moore as his literary executors. After noting that Griswold himself had burned three trunkfuls of his papers just before he died, Wallace goes on to say, "A vast number of them I presume we shall burn."

Chapter One

1. *Art, Scenery and Philosophy in Europe* (Philadelphia: Herman Hooker, 1855), p. viii. Subsequent printed accounts of Wallace's life tend to be based on this "Memoir," as well as on Horace Binney's "Obituary," which follows in the prefatory matter. A frequently repeated error, for example, that Wallace went to Europe in 1849, seems to stem from a misreading of the following sentence in the "Memoir": "After the death of his mother on the 9th July, 1849, Mr. Wallace resolved to pass some time in Europe, and embarking in April of the following year, spent a twelvemonth in England, Germany, France and Italy" (p. xvii). Unless otherwise indicated, the "Memoir" serves for my basic source throughout this chapter.

2. For a brief life of John W. Wallace, see Henry Flanders, "A Commemorative Address . . . on John William Wallace . . ., *Pennsylvania Magazine of History and Biography*, 8 (1884), ix-xliv.

3. See Paul D. Evans, *The Holland Land Company, Buffalo Historical Society Publications*, 28 (1924), 169 - 76.

4. Quoted by Flanders, p. xix.

5. Ms. letter, Historical Society of Pennsylvania.

6. Quoted by Flanders, p. xvi.

7. "Memoir," p. ix. Quoted by Flanders, p. xvi.

8. Ms. letter, Jan. 19, 1827, University of Virginia.

9. Ms. letter, Sept. 11, 1829, Historical Society of Pennsylvania.

10. Ms. letter, Sept. 18, 1830, Historical Society of Pennsylvania.

11. *A Philadelphia Perspective: The Diary of Sidney George Fisher . . . 1834 - 1871*, ed. Nicholas B. Wainwright (Philadelphia: Historical Society of Pennsylvania, 1967), p. 152. In subsequent years Fisher made similar entries about Horace Binney.

12. Binney quoted by Charles C. Binney, *The Life of Horace Binney* (Philadelphia and London: Lippincott, 1903), p. 266.

13. Ms. copy of letter, Jan. 29, 1845, University of Virginia.

14. Asahel C. Kendrick, *The Life and Letters of Mrs. Emily C. Judson* (New York: Sheldon, 1860), p. 136.

15. Edward P. Cheyney, *History of the University of Pennsylvania, 1740 - 1940* (Philadelphia: University of Pennsylvania Press, 1940), pp. 225 - 26.

16. Ms. letter, Historical Society of Pennsylvania.

17. "Horace Binney Wallace," *Nassau Literary Magazine*, 19 (Oct., 1858), 66 - 68. A copy at the Princeton University Library bears the pencilled name "Kenyon" as author.

18. *Ibid.*, p. 68.

19. Flanders, pp. xl - xlii.

20. Ms. letter, Feb. 11, 1853, Massachusetts Historical Society. Although it is catalogued as addressed to R. H. Dana, Jr., the personal tone

relates this letter more convincingly to those that John Wallace is known to have written to the elder Dana.

21. That John Wallace "wrote in stilted phrases" and adorned "his statements of fact with extraneous bits of information" sometimes to the detriment of fact is developed by Charles Fairman in *The Oliver Wendell Holmes Devise History of the Supreme Court of the United States,* VI, *Reconstruction and Reunion, 1864 - 1888* (New York and London: Macmillan, 1971), Part One, pp. 72 - 76. The "stilted phrases" certainly appear in the "Memoir."

22. Ms. letter to R. H. Dana, Jr., Jan. 28, 1853, Massachusetts Historical Society.

23. G. E. Hatvary, "The Wallace-Griswold Correspondence," *Boston Public Library Quarterly,* 8 (Jan., 1956), 7. (Hereafter referred to as "Correspondence.")

24. Flanders, p. xl.

25. See note 1 for Chapter 2 for full documentation.

26. Vol. 8 (Nov., 1836), 605 - 12. *LC,* pp. 103 - 17.

27. *LC,* pp. 99 - 100. Not a review. *Stanley,* I, 216 - 21.

28. Ms. letter, Aug. 13, 1840, University of Virginia.

29. *The Letters of Edgar Allan Poe,* ed. John Ostrom (Cambridge: Harvard University Press, 1948), I, 174. (Hereafter referred to as *Letters.*)

30. *Graham's Magazine,* 19 (Nov., 1841). *The Complete Works of Edgar Allan Poe,* ed. James Harrison (New York: Crowell, 1902), XV, 198. (Hereafter referred to as *Works.*). The word "affectation" did not have a necessarily pejorative connotation in Poe's time. As for "pedantic," Wallace himself called an early article of his "Scraps from the Notebook of a Pedant."

31. "Memoir," p. xvii.

32. Ms. copy of letter, Sept. 30 (added in another hand: "1843"), University of Virginia.

33. Ms. copy of letter, Nov. 3, 1844, University of Virginia.

34. *Graham's,* 26 (Jan., 1845), 1. *LC,* p. 403.

35. *Ibid.,* p. 4. Not in *LC.*

36. *LC,* p. 400. The Preface, "To the Reader," not in *Graham's.*

37. *LC,* p. 399. I have not been able to determine "Henry's" identity.

38. "George P. Morris," *Graham's,* 26 (Apr., 1845), 145 - 50. *LC,* pp. 205 - 24. Also, as Introduction to George P. Morris, *Poems* (New York: Scribner, 1860).

39. An introductory note to "Contributions to the Ephemeral Press" (*ASE,* p. 293) speaks of Wallace as "holding no connexions of office or profit whatsoever with the public press."

40. *LC,* 2nd ed. (1856), p. 224. The date given here for this letter as Aug. 2, 1848, is erroneous, since Wallace's review appeared in the *Home Journal* on Jan. 8 and 15, 1848.

41. Ms. letter to Prof. John Maclean, Nov. 3, 1838, Princeton University.

42. Ms. copy (?) of letter, Feb. 18, 1840, Historical Society of Pennsylvania.

43. Ms. copy of letter to Prof. Joseph Henry, Nov. 19, 1844, University of Virginia.

44. Ms. letters to R. H. Dana, Sr. and R. H. Dana, Jr., 1849 - 50, Massachusetts Historical Society.

45. See note 22.

46. Review of *ASPE*, *Putnam's Monthly*, 6 (Sept., 1855). Repr. Parke Godwin, *Out of the Past: Critical and Literary Papers* (New York: Putnam, 1870), p. 307.

47. "Obituary," *ASPE*, p. xxvii.

48. See note 22.

49. See note 20.

50. See note 22.

51. See note 28.

52. Ms. copy of letter to "Miss" Goddard, Jan. 25, 1845, University of Virginia.

53. Kendrick, p. 136.

54. "Correspondence," p. 6.

55. *LC*, p. 191. As noted in the Preface, Wallace's diary is now lost.

56. Kendrick, p. 158.

57. Kendrick, p. 162.

58. *Knickerbocker Magazine*, 26 (Aug., 1850). Repr. *HJ*, 6 (Sept. 28, 1850). *LC*, pp. 242, 234.

59. "Correspondence," p. 19.

60. Howard R. Marraro, "American Travelers in Rome, 1811 - 1850," *Catholic Historical Review*, 29 (Jan., 1944), 509.

61. "An American in England," *HJ*, 7 (Nov. 15, 1851). Signed, "An Outsider." *ASE*, p. 132. Textual references are made, whenever possible, to this more easily accessible volume, rather than to its predecessor, *ASPE*.

62. Boston and New York: Houghton, Mifflin, 1899, p. 198.

63. Ms. letter, Julia W. Howe to Edward Twistleton, Apr. 20, 1853, Houghton Library, Harvard University.

64. I am indebted to Deborah Clifford for this observation; also for bringing to my attention three letters in which Julia Ward Howe speaks of Wallace after his death. Mrs. Howe speaks of her lack of rapport with her children in the one she wrote to Auguste Comte on Feb. 13, 1853. (Houghton Library, Harvard University.)

65. Ms. letter, Julia W. Howe to Louisa Crawford, Feb. 18, 1853, Houghton Library, Harvard University.

66. Besides her unsent letter to Wallace at the end of this chapter, see her letter to Comte, note 64.

67. See Phyllis Blanchard, "A Psycho-analytical Study of Auguste Comte," *American Journal of Psychology*, 29 (Apr., 1918), 159 - 81.

68. "First Visit to Comte," *HJ*, 11 (Mar. 14, 1855).

69. Five hundred francs paid about one third of the yearly rent for Comte's apartment. R. L. Hawkins, *Auguste Comte and the United States (1816 - 1853)* (Cambridge: Harvard University Press, 1936), p. 56.

70. "Memoir," p. xviii.

71. Ms. letter, Aug. 7, 1851, Historical Society of Pennsylvania.

72. See note 20.

73. Ms. letter to R. H. Dana, Sr., Aug. 30, 1855, Massachusetts Historical Society.

74. Hawthorne and Godwin quoted in Albert F. McLean, Jr., *William Cullen Bryant* (New York: Twayne, 1964), p. 23.

75. Ms. letter to John Wallace, Nov. 25, 1852, Historical Society of Pennsylvania. The meeting is also mentioned by Parke Godwin, *Life of William Cullen Bryant* (New York: Appleton, 1883), II, 65.

76. On Nov. 16, 1840, Prof. Samuel Miller of Princeton replied to an inquiry by John Wallace, stating that he could give no information about a "worthy ancestor" (Ms. letter, Historical Society of Pennsylvania). See John Bernard Burke, *Royal Descents and Pedigrees of Founders' Kin* (London: Harrison, 1864), Pedigree XVI; *A Genealogical and Heraldic Dictionary* . . . , 7th ed. (London: Hurst and Blackett, 1854), pp. 720 - 21; and *A Visitation of the Seats and Arms* . . . , 2nd. Ser. (London: Hurst and Blackett, 1854), I, 31 - 33.

77. "Memoir," pp. xix - xx.

78. Auguste Comte, *Confessions and Testament,* ed. Albert Crompton (Liverpool: H. Young, 1908), p. 425.

79. "Memoir," p. xx.

80. *Galignani's Messenger,* Dec. 20, 1852. The report reads: "Mr. Binney Wallace [sic], an American literary man, cut his throat on Thursday, in his apartment in the Hotel des Bains, Rue St. Lazare. It is said that he had exhibited symptoms of insanity."

81. I am indebted for this opinion to the medical historians Peter H. Niebyl, M.D. and Jacques M. Quen, M.D.

82. See note 20.

83. Charles J. F. Binney, *Genealogy of the Binney Family in the United States* (Albany, N.Y.: Munsell's sons, 1886), p. 60.

84. See note 4.

85. *New York Mirror,* 13 (Mar. 12, 1836), 292 - 93.

86. Titled *Autobiography* (unpublished), II, entry for Jan. 7, 1853, Historical Society of Pennsylvania.

87. Ms. letter, Houghton Library, Harvard University. Somewhat abridged in G. E. Hatvary, "Horace Binney Wallace: A Study in Self-Destruction," *Princeton University Library Chronicle,* 25 (Winter, 1964), 148 - 49. Wallace called Julia Howe "Glaukópis," Athena's epithet in the *Odyssey.*

88. Letter to Comte. (See note 64.)

89. *Ibid.*

90. See note 65.

91. *Words for the Hour* (Boston: Ticknor and Fields, 1857), pp. 52 - 56. Partially quoted in *Reminiscences*, pp. 200 - 201.

Chapter Two

1. Vol. 13 (Dec. 5, 1835), 180 - 81; (Dec. 19, 1835), 197; (Jan. 30, 1836), 245; (May 14, 1836), 365, respectively.

2. *New York Mirror*, 14 (Apr. 15, 1837), 336.

3. See note 26 for Chapter 1.

4. Jack Simmons, *Southey* (London: Collins, 1945), p. 195.

5. *Southern Literary Messenger*, 2 (July, 1936); *Works*, IX, 69.

6. In reprinting Binney's "Obituary" in *ASPE*, John Wallace eliminated two references to his brother's novel. (See note 14 for Chapter 7.)

7. Vol. 16, 54 - 57; *LC*, pp. 384 - 92.

8. Vol. 15 (Aug., 1856), 484 - 86; *LC*, pp. 379 - 84.

9. Vol. 2, 217 - 19; *LC*, pp. 392 - 98.

10. Review in *Hesperian*, 2 (Mar., 1839), 409 - 10.

11. The heading of the *Hesperian* review adds: "Columbus: Isaac N. Whiting, 1838." There appeared also a London edition, by Wiley and Putnam, in 1839.

12. Vol. 10 (Dec., 1838), 99.

13. Vol. 1 (Dec. 8, 1838), 11.

14. Vol. 6 (Dec. 22, 1838), 221.

15. Vol. 4 (Jan., 1839), 239.

16. Vol. 4 (Jan., 1839), 65.

17. See note 30 for Chapter 1.

18. See Agnes M. Sibley, *Alexander Pope's Prestige in America, 1725 - 1835* (New York; King's Crown Press, 1949); William E. Leonard, *Byron and Byronism in America, Columbia University Studies in English*, ser. II, vol. 1, no. 1 (New York, 1907); and Annabel Newton, *Wordsworth in Early American Criticism* (Chicago: University of Chicago Press, 1928).

19. The text of the five dialogues in *LC* (pp. 245 - 378) is presumably their original version. In incorporating the first four ("A Dialogue by the Sea," "A Dinner-Party Dialogue," "A Dialogue in a Library," and the first "A Dialogue in Travelling") into *Stanley*, Wallace made relatively few changes. They form Chapters 5 and 10 of Volume I and Chapters 1 (in part) and 3 of Volume II, respectively.

20. There was widespread belief at this time in America of Pope's virtuous life. See Sibley, Ch. 2.

21. Harriet Shelley's suicide was not generally known in America at this time.

22. The ambivalent attitude Wallace inherited toward Byron is illustrated by an anonymous article in the *North American Review*, 20 (Jan., 1825), 1 - 47, lamenting the poet's death. After some forty pages of praise,

the writer concludes by wishing that Byron's works could be removed forever from public view.

23. Letter to Hiram Ketcham, Feb. 22, 1849, quoted in the front matter of *ASPE* and *LC*.

24. For a discussion of the Aristotelian emphasis on the difference between fact and probability prevalent in American criticism at this time, see William Charvat, *Origins of American Critical Thought*, 1810 - 1835 (Philadelphia: University of Pennsylvania Press, 1836), Ch. 7.

25. For a discussion of Scottish influence on American criticism, see *ibid.*, Ch. 3.

26. "The Dynamo and the Virgin," Ch. 25, *The Education of Henry Adams* (Boston and New York: Houghton, Mifflin, 1918).

27. "Letter to B—," *Works*, VII, xxxvii.

28. See note 6.

29. *Henry Pulteney, or the Adventures of a Wanderer, Burton's Gentleman's Magazine*, 2 (Jan.-June, 1838), 3 (July-Aug., 1838), 4 (Jan.-June, 1839). The Jan.-Mar., 1838, installments appeared anonymously; those following carried "William Landor." (For pp., see Bibliography.)

30. June 1, 1838.

31. In *LC*, the second "A Dialogue in Travelling." These two dialogues, as well as the setting of *Henry Pulteney*, suggest that Wallace spent some time in Europe before 1838, but there is no other evidence.

32. See note 85 for Chapter 1.

33. *Ibid.*, 14 (Jan. 14, 1837), 229.

34. *Godey's Lady's Book*, 16 (Mar., 1838), 125 - 35. Unsigned, but the Feb. issue (p. 96) announced this story as written by the author of "A Sermon in a Garden."

35. *Godey's*, 20 (Feb., 1840), 77 - 80.

36. *Godey's*, 21 (Nov., 1840), 225 - 30.

37. *Burton's*, 7 (Nov., 1840), 256 - 64.

38. *Godey's*, 22 (Mar., 1841), 128 - 33. Identified as by "W. Landor" in the April issue (p. 192).

39. *Graham's*, 19 (July, 1841), 19 - 26.

40. *Godey's*, 24 (Mar., 1842), 158 - 65.

41. *Graham's*, 26 (Apr., 1845), 176 - 84.

42. Vol. 4 (Apr., 1839), 241 - 42; 5 (Aug., 1839), 96; (Nov., 1839), 236.

43. Vol. 7 (Sept., 1840), 151 - 52; (Oct., 1840), 201 - 22; (Nov., 1840), 249 - 50.

44. *Graham's*, 26 (Jan. 1845), 1 - 4; (Apr., 1845), 168 - 70; 28 (Apr., 1846), 153 - 57. *LC*, pp. 399 - 438.

Chapter Three

1. For the most detailed and scholarly biography of Poe, see Arthur H. Quinn, *Edgar Allan Poe: A Critical Biography* (New York; Appleton-Century-Crofts, 1941). For a concise, somewhat more up-to-date, and less

sentimental record of Poe's life, see Thomas O. Mabbott, "Annals," in *Poems*, Vol. I of *Collected Works of Edgar Allan Poe* (Cambridge: Harvard University Press, 1969).

2. See G. E. Hatvary, "Poe's Borrowings from H. B. Wallace," *American Literature*, 38 (Nov., 1966), 365 - 72.

3. This was called to my attention by J. J. Cohane.

4. See *À Rebours* (Paris: Charpentier, 1884, etc.), *passim*.

5. Credit is due for this observation to J. J. Cohane.

6. *Works*, V, 33; *Stanley*, II, 78; *LC*, p. 338.

7. *Stanley*, I, 206 - 7; *Works* V, 44 - 45.

8. *Letters*, I, 239.

9. Robert D. Jacobs, *Poe: Journalist and Critic* (Baton Rouge: Louisiana State University Press, 1969), p. 122.

10. *Letters*, I, 174.

11. Vol. 25, 145 - 48. *LC*, pp. 38 - 45.

12. *Letters*, I, 246.

13. *Doings of Gotham . . .*, ed. Jacob E. Spannuth and T. O. Mabbott (Pottsville, Pa: Spannuth, 1929), pp. 68, 74. See also p. 34.

14. See note 38 for Chapter 1.

15. Vol. 1 (Apr. 5, 1845), 220 - 21. Not in *Works*, but the style and tone appear to be Poe's.

16. Vol. 1 (Jan. 13 and 14, 1845).

17. Vol. 1 (Mar. 8, Mar. 15, Mar. 22, Mar. 29, Apr. 5, 1845).

18. *Doings of Gotham*, p. 68. Poe writes: "The real author (Mr. Landor), although a man of high talent, has a certain set of phrases which cannot easily be mistaken."

19. *Letters*, II, 415 - 16.

20. *Letters*, II, 441.

21. *Letters*, II, 437.

22. *Works of the Late Edgar A. Poe* (New York: Redfield, 1850 - 56), III, xxxi.

23. Burton R. Pollin makes a similar suggestion in *Discoveries in Poe* (Notre Dame and London: University of Notre Dame Press, 1970), pp. 159 and 275.

24. Killis Campbell's concluding words in "The Poe-Griswold Controversy," *The Mind of Poe and Other Studies* (1933; repr. New York: Russell and Russell, 1962), p. 98.

25. "Rufus Wilmot Griswold," *University of Texas Studies in English*, No. 5 (Oct. 8, 1925), 101 - 65; *Rufus Wilmot Griswold: Poe's Literary Executor* (Nashville, Tenn.: Vanderbilt University Press, 1943).

26. *New England Quarterly*, 16 (Dec., 1943), 670 - 72.

27. *Passages from the Correspondence . . . of . . . Griswold*, ed. William M. Griswold (Cambridge, Mass.: W. M. Griswold, 1898), p. 5.

28. *Ibid.*, p. 7.

29. Bayless, p. 10.

30. Griswold to R. H. Dana, Sr., quoted by Bayless, p. 66.

31. Quinn, p. 692; Bayless, 157 - 8; Mabbott, see note 26, p. 672.

32. Bayless, p. 108.

33. See note 23.

34. In a letter to E. A. Duyckinck in 1846, Griswold speaks of "the brutal article" that had appeared in the *N. Y. Mirror* about Poe: "I who have as much cause as any man to quarrel with Poe, would sooner have cut off my hand than used it to write such an ungentlemanly card, though every word were true. But my indignation at [?] this treatment even of an enemy exceeds my power of expression." New York Public Library.

35. The phrase is Quinn's, p. 350.

36. Charles F. Briggs to James R. Lowell, quoted by Campbell, p. 66.

37. See Charles K. Imbrie, et al., *Biography of the Class of 1835 of the College of New Jersey* (Newark: Ward and Tichenor, 1888), p. 83: "In a letter to the writer of this paragraph, Dr. [O. W.?] Holmes said in 1885: 'I remember Rufus W. Griswold saying to me, that of the persons whose intellect he had envied, your Class mate, Wallace, was the one who stood foremost.' "

38. Philadelphia, 1845. First publication of the review unknown. *LC*, pp. 121 - 24.

39. See Perry Miller, *The Raven and the Whale* (New York: Harcourt, Brace, 1956) and Sidney P. Moss, *Poe's Literary Battles* (Durham, N.C.: Duke University Press, 1963).

40. Miller, p. 195.

41. Vol. 30 (Oct., Nov., 1847), 342 - 45, 441 - 45; 31 (Feb., Mar., Apr., 1848), 162 - 64, 254 - 57, 348 - 51.

42. Vol. 16 (Apr., 1850), 231 - 40.

43. "Correspondence," p. 7.

44. *Ibid.*

45. New York: Baker and Scribner, 1847.

46. Wallace's essay was reprinted together with one by John M. Mackie as *The Military and Civil Life of George Washington* (New York: William Graham, 1849). Its partial reprinting in *ASE*, pp. 443 - 51, is the best proof of its sometimes questioned authorship.

47. Ms. letter from Simms to Griswold, July 15, 1847, Boston Public Library.

48. Bayless, p. 279.

49. *Ibid.*

50. Ms. letter, New York Public Library.

51. *Ibid.* The identity of "Junius" as Wallace is revealed by a scrap of paper enclosed in Griswold's letter to George L. Duyckinck, Apr. 9, 1855, New York Public Library.

52. Vol. 23 (July, 1848), 59.

53. "Correspondence," p. 8.

54. *Ibid.*, p. 9.

55. *Ibid.*, p. 10.
56. *Ibid.*, pp. 9 - 10.
57. Ms. letter, Oct. 31, 1849, Massachusetts Historical Society.
58. "Correspondence," p. 13.
59. *Ibid.*, p. 14. The reference is to Willis's controversy with a *N. Y. Tribune* correspondent, "Quispiam," over the American Art Union, in the course of which "Quispiam" called Willis a profligate. Wallace's sympathetic attitude toward Willis makes his unkind criticism in the revised version of his review of Griswold's *Prose Writers of America* especially puzzling.
60. See note 25, p. 670.
61. Part VIII, Ch. 4.
62. "Correspondence," p. 15.
63. Vol. 26, 162 - 72; signed "J.H.M.," standing for "John H. Meredith," the name Wallace used in corresponding with William Graham. Repr. *HJ*, 6 (Sept. 28, 1850); *LC*, pp. 225 - 43.
64. "Correspondence," p. 17.
65. *Ibid.*, p. 19.
66. *Ibid.*, p. 17.
67. See note 22.
68. "Correspondence," p. 19.
69. Ms. letter, Historical Society of Pennsylvania.
70. Ms. letter, July 9, 1862, Massachusetts Historical Society.

Chapter Four

1. Ms. letter, Sept. 15, 1836, Historical Society of Pennsylvania.
2. Ms. letter from L. M. Sargent to Susan B. Wallace, Aug. 20, 1841, Historical Society of Pennsylvania.
3. *Dictionary of American Biography* (New York: Scribner, 1928 - 37).
4. *The Formative Era of American Law* (Boston: Little, Brown, 1939), pp. 144 - 59.
5. Philadelphia: J.S. Littell, and New York: Halsted and Voorhies, 1838 - 40; second ed., London: A. Maxwell, 1841 - 42. Wallace and Hare based their edition on the latter.
6. The publishers for this set and all subsequent legal editions by Wallace and Hare were Topliff and J. W. Johnson, in Philadelphia.
7. An indication of Wallace's earnings is given by a letter from him to T. and J. W. Johnson on Sept. 12, 1848, asking $1. 25 for himself and Hare for each copy of the new edition printed. Also, he wishes the editors to retain the copyright. In a letter to the Johnsons on Mar. 20, 1848, Wallace asks $250.00 flat fee for editing a volume. (Ms. letters, Historical Society of Pennsylvania.)
8. Vol. 9, new ser. 2 (Nov., 1849), 239 - 40.
9. First publication unknown. The piece may have appeared in an issue of the *National Press* no longer extant. *LC*, pp. 147 - 48.

10. Beginning with the Nov. 21, 1846, issue. In 1901, the *Home Journal* became the *Town and Country.*

11. *HJ*, 3 (July 29, 1848); *ASE*, p. 321.

12. *HJ*, 7 (Aug. 5, 1851); *ASE*, pp. 322 - 24.

13. *HJ*, 7 (Sept. 2, 1851); *ASE*, pp. 325 - 26.

14. *HJ*, 7 (Aug. 16, 1851); *ASE*, p. 330.

15. *HJ*, 3 (July 8, 1848); *ASE*, pp. 355 - 57.

16. *NP*, 1 (Sept. 26, 1846); signed "J.K." *ASE*, p. 353.

17. *NP*, 1 (Sept. 26, 1846); signed "R.B." *ASE*, p. 346.

18. *HJ*, 3 (July 22, 1848); *ASE*, titled "Midsummer Congress," p. 345.

19. *HJ*, 7 (Aug. 30, 1851; *ASE*, p. 351.

20. *NP*, 1 (Oct. 17, 1846); *ASE*, p. 295.

21. *HJ*, 7 (Aug. 23, 1851); *ASE*, pp. 296 - 97.

22. *HJ*, 3 (July 15, 1848); *ASE*, pp. 312 - 13.

23. *NP*, 1 (Oct. 17, 1846); *LC*, pp. 26 - 29.

24. *HJ*, 3 (July 29, 1848); *LC*, pp. 29 - 32.

25. *HJ*, 3 (Oct. 28, 1848); *ASE*, pp. 303 - 304.

26. *HJ*, 3 (Oct. 21, 1848); *ASE*, p. 300.

27. *HJ*, 7 (Oct. 25, 1851); *ASE*, pp. 316 - 17.

28. *HJ*, 7 (Aug. 23, 1851); *ASE*, p. 309.

29. *NP*, 1 (Oct. 17, 1846); *LC*, pp. 93 - 94.

30. *HJ*, 3 (Aug. 4, 1848); *LC*, pp. 92, 95.

31. *HJ*, 8 (Jan. 3, 1852); *ASE*, p. 372.

32. First publication unknown. *ASE*, p. 369.

33. *HJ*, 7 (Nov. 29, 1851); *ASE*, pp. 363 - 65.

34. *NP*, 1 (Nov. 7, 1846); *ASE*, pp. 366 - 67.

35. *HJ*, 3 (Sept. 2, 1848); *ASE*, pp. 360 - 62.

36. Burlington, N.J., 1849; repr. Philadelphia, 1855.

37. *HJ*, 7 (Aug. 30, 1851); *ASE*, pp. 358 - 60.

38. *HJ*, 3 (July 22, 1848); *ASE*, titled "Conclusion of the Mexican War. 1848," p. 406.

39. *HJ*, 4 (Jan. 6, 1849); *ASE*, p. 426.

40. See note 9. *ASE*, pp. 441 - 42.

41. *HJ*, 3 (July 8, 1848); *ASE*, pp. 412 - 15.

42. First publication unknown. *ASE*, p. 425.

43. *HJ*, 3 (July 15, 1848); *ASE*, p. 429.

44. *HJ*, 3 (Aug. 12, 1848); *ASE*, titled "France and the Man," pp. 431 - 32.

45. *HJ*, 7 (Nov. 1, 1851); *ASE*, titled "American Interference in Europe. 1851," p. 411.

46. *HJ*, 3 (Aug. 19, 1848); *ASE*, pp. 397 - 400.

47. "The Great Exhibition—London," signed "J.A.," *HJ*, 7 (Aug. 2, 1851); *ASE*, pp. 197 - 215.

48. *HJ*, 7 (Aug. 9, 1851); *ASE*, p. 386.

49. *HJ*, 7 (Sept. 20, 1851); *ASE*, titled "The Victory at Cowes," p. 392.

50. *HJ*, 8 (Jan. 17, 1852); *ASE*, titled "Another View of the Question," p. 394.

51. *HJ*, 4 (Jan. 27, 1849); *ASE*, pp. 376 - 78.

52. *HJ*, 7 (Oct. 11, 1851); *ASE*, p. 383.

53. *HJ*, 7 (Nov. 8, 1851); *ASE*, p. 401.

54. See note 47. *ASE*, pp. 202 - 3.

55. Louisville, Ky.: Morton and Griswold, 1847. *HJ*, 3 (Jan. 8 and Jan. 15, 1848); *LC*, pp. 195 - 204.

56. New York: Paine and Burgess, 1846. *NP*, 1 (Feb. 21, 1846); *LC*, pp. 191 - 95.

57. *NP*, 1 (May 9, 1846). Not a review, signed, "A New Contributor." *LC*, pp. 60 - 63.

58. *Forest Leaves* (Philadelphia: Lindsay and Blakison, 1845). *NP*, 1 (Sept. 26, 1846); *LC*, pp. 55 - 56. The name is misspelled as "Pearson."

59. Philadelphia: T. K. and P. G. Collins, 1839. *NP*, 1 (Feb. 21, 1846); *LC*, pp. 56 - 60.

60. New York: Wiley and Putnam, 1845. See note 9. *LC*, pp. 164 - 73.

61. London: P. Bentley, 1845. See note 9. *LC*, pp. 129 - 34.

62. London: J. R. Smith, 1820. See note 9. *LC*, pp. 134 - 38.

63. New York, 1845. In part, *NP*, 1 (Feb. 14, 1846); *LC*, pp. 141 - 46.

64. George Gibbs, *Memoirs of the Administrations of Washington and John Adams, edited from the Papers of Oliver Wolcott* . . . (New York: Van Norden, 1846). *Graham's*, 29 (Aug., 1846), 108. Repr. *NP*, 1 (Oct. 17, 1846), signed "A Federalist." In an editorial note G. P. Morris disclaims endorsement of "the opinions of the writer—who belongs to a school of politics in direct opposition to our own." *LC*, pp. 63 - 66.

65. *The Life of the Rev. Joseph White. Written by Himself* . . ., ed. John H. Thom (London: J. Chapman, 1845). See note 9. *LC*, pp. 150 - 53.

66. *Miscellaneous Sermons* (Philadelphia: Carey and Hart, 1846). *NP*, 1 (Mar. 7, 1846); *LC*, pp. 153 - 55.

67. Boston: J. Munroe, 1838 - 39. *NP*, 1 (Mar. 7, 1846); *LC*, pp. 156 - 58.

68. Eng. trans. New York: J. and H. Langley, 1846. See note 9. *LC*, pp. 117 - 21.

69. Thomas H. James, anonymous author (London: J. Ollivier, 1846). *NP*, 1 (Apr. 11, 1846); *LC*, abridged, pp. 162 - 64.

70. Philadelphia: Lea and Blanchard, 1845. See note 9. *LC*, pp. 124 - 28.

71. New York: Appleton, 1845. See note 9. *LC*, pp. 139 - 41.

72. New York: Appleton, 1846 - 47. *NP*, 1 (Apr. 11, 1846); *LC*, abridged, pp. 158 - 59.

73. *An Author's Mind* (Philadelphia, Carey and Hart, 1847). See note 9. *LC*, pp. 160 - 61.

74. Philadelphia (?), 1848. *NP*, 1 (Oct. 10, 1846). Not a review, signed "J.K." *LC*, pp. 187 - 91.

75. See "Correspondence," pp. 17, 19. *Sartain's,* 7 (Nov., 1850), 288 - 98. The signature, "William Landor"—unusual for 1850—was probably supplied by Griswold. *LC,* pp. 67 - 91. The payment is mentioned in John Sartain, *The Reminiscenses of a Very Old Man, 1808 - 1897* (New York: Appleton, 1899), p. 220.

76. *HJ,* 7 (Sep. 6, 1851), *ASE,* pp. 336 - 37.

77. *NP,* 1 (Oct. 17, 1846) and *HJ,* 3 (Aug. 19, 1848); *ASE,* pp. 333 - 35.

78. First publication unknown. *LC,* pp. 454 - 57.

79. First publication unknown. *LC,* pp. 451 - 53.

80. "Mr. Macready," *HJ,* 3 (July 29, 1848); *LC,* p. 440.

81. *HJ,* 3 (Sept. 9, 1848); *ASE,* pp. 338 - 42.

Chapter Five

1. *ASE,* p. 2. Textual references are made to this more easily accessible volume rather than to its predecessor, *ASPE.*

2. See Lionello Venturi, *History of Art Criticism* (New York: Dutton, 1936), Ch. 8.

3. R. E. Spiller et al., 3rd rev. ed. (New York: Macmillan, 1963), pp. 829 - 30.

4. "Letter from Florence," *HJ,* 7 (Aug. 9, 1851), signed "J.A."

5. "Horace Bender" [pseud.], *The Travels . . . of a Yankee Stonecutter* (New York: Putnam, 1852).

6. See Venturi, *History of Art Criticism,* Chs. 9 and 11.

7. *The Works of John Ruskin,* ed. E. T. Cook and A. Wedderburn (London and New York: G. Allen, 1903 - 12), III, 571 - 72.

8. *Ibid.,* XII, 341 - 93.

9. Anthony Blunt, *Artistic Theory in Italy, 1450 - 1600* (Oxford: Clarendon Press, 1940), p. 34.

10. *The Works of Walter Pater* (London: Macmillan, 1900 - 1), I, 125.

11. W. E. Suida, ed., *Raphael* (New York: Phaidon, 1941), pp. 6 and 32.

12. See Bernard Berenson, *The Central Italian Painters of the Renaissance,* 2nd ed. (New York and London: Putnam's sons, 1909), pp. 100 ff.

13. *A Short History of Italian Art* (New York: Macmillan, 1926), pp. 279 - 80.

14. See note 4.

15. *HJ,* 7 (Oct. 4, 1851), signed "J.A."

16. *HJ,* 7 (Nov. 8, 1851), signed "J.A."

17. *HJ,* 11 (Apr. 28, 1855).

Chapter Six

1. Vol. 36, 4th Ser. 6 (Jan., 1854), 136 - 42; *ASPE,* pp. 331 - 45.

2. *Lettres d' Auguste Comte à divers* (Paris: Fonds typographic de . . . A.C., 1902 - 5), I¹, 47; *Correspondance inédite d'Auguste Comte* (Paris:

Société positiviste, 1903 - 4), I, 240 - 41; III, 110 - 11; *Lettres inédites à C. de Blignières* (Paris: Vrin, 1932), p. 29; *Nouvelles lettres inédites, Archives positivistes* (Paris, 1939), p. 224.

3. *Nouvelles lettres inédites*, p. 224.
4. Cambridge: Harvard University Press, 1936.
5. Comte, *Synthèse subjective* (Paris: Chez l'auteur, 1856), I, liv. Also Hawkins, pp. 50 - 51.
6. *Lettres . . . à divers*, I¹, 71 - 72.
7. Ms. letter, La Maison d' Auguste Comte, Paris.
8. Vol. 34, 4th Ser. 4, 9 - 37.
9. See note 1.
10. Paris: L. Mathias, 1851 - 54, II, xxv. The reference to Wallace is made in a letter from Comte to M'Clintock printed here.
11. "Correspondence," pp. 22 - 24.
12. *Ibid.*, pp. 21 - 22.
13. *Lettres . . . a divers*, I¹, 172.
14. See note 78 for Chapter 1.
15. *Ibid.*, p. 432. Quoted by Hawkins, p. 53.
16. Ms. letter, Nov. 26, 1853, La Maison d'Auguste Comte.
17. I was told some years ago of the existence of a copy of *ASPE* at the Maison d'Auguste Comte. John Wallace may have presented it to Comte in person, for there exists a letter at the Maison from J. W. Wallace to Comte, written in Paris on Sept. 11, 1857, expressing a desire to call on Comte.
18. According to Hawkins, Comte "read English with ease, but could not speak it" (p. 6).
19. Hawkins, p. 59.
20. Quoted by Hawkins, p. 53.

Chapter Seven

1. Ms. draft, undated, Boston Public Library.
2. *ASPE*, p. xxi. The fragmentary essay, "The Roman Forum," for example, appears to John Wallace to be the last piece written by his brother—presumably from notes taken on the scene—showing "the mark of having been written with physical difficulty and pain" (*ASE*, p. 183).
3. "Correspondence," p. 20.
4. *Words for the Hour*, p. 49.
5. "Correspondence," p. 21. Hooker simply writes "R.H. Dana."
6. Ms. letter, Dec. 6, 1854, Boston Public Library.
7. On Jan. 6, 1855, Hooker complained to Griswold that the New York press was neglecting the book, although fifty copies had been sent to the press. ("Correspondence," p. 20.)
8. Vol. 13 (May, 1855), 312 - 16.
9. Vol. 81 (July, 1855), 212 - 44.
10. *Putnam's Monthly*, 5 (June, 1855), 576. Unsigned; identified in *HJ*, 11 (June 16, 1855).

11. See note 46 for Chapter 1, pp. 302 - 3.

12. Vol. 11 (Mar. 3, 10, 24, Apr. 14, 28, May 12, June 16, July 21, Aug. 11, 1855).

13. Ms. letter, Historical Society of Pennsylvania.

14. There can be little doubt that John Wallace did a disservice to his brother's literary reputation by maintaining the secrecy of his authorship of *Stanley*. In 1867, for example, Thomas Wentworth Higginson wrote in a copy of *Stanley* (now at the Harvard College Library): "After a long search for this remarkable book (which I read when a boy) I found it at last in Chicago." Higginson's further notations demonstrate Wallace's authorship, of which apparently not many readers were aware.

15. Vol. 12 (Mar. 8, 22, 29, Apr. 5, May 17, June 7, Oct. 4, 18, Nov. 8, 29, 1856).

16. Ms. letter, May 23, 1856, Massachusetts Historical Society. Parry and McMillan brought out a second edition of *LC* in 1856.

17. Vol. 37 (May, 1856), 428 - 29.

18. Vol. 48, 76 - 79.

19. Philadelphia: Lippincott, 1868.

20. Ms. letter, Massachusetts Historical Society.

21. Ms. letter, Feb. 11, 1908, Princeton University.

22. My correspondence with Col. Ward.

23. See note 3 for Chapter 5.

24. New York, 1947, pp. 37 - 38, 202.

25. Norman: University of Oklahoma Press, pp. 90, 96 - 97, 104, 110.

Selected Bibliography

PRIMARY SOURCES

1. Fiction

Stanley, or the Recollections of a Man of the World. 2 vols. Philadelphia: Lea and Blanchard, 1838; London: Wiley and Putnam, 1839.

Henry Pulteney, or the Adventures of a Wanderer. Burton's Gentleman's Magazine, 2 (Jan.-June, 1838), 40 - 46, 89 - 98, 183 - 91, 257 - 64, 312 - 19, 393 - 98; 3 (July-Aug., 1838), 51 - 53, 128 - 34; '4 (Jan.-June, 1839), 19 - 26, 94 - 101, 169 - 76, 220 - 26, 287 - 90, 330 - 36.

"Confessions of a Dreamer," *New York Mirror,* 13 (Mar. 12, 1836), 292 - 93.

"An Incident at La Trappe," *New York Mirror,* 14 (Jan. 14, 1837), 229.

"The Victims of Passion." *Godey's Lady's Book,* 16 (Mar., 1838), 125 - 35.

"The Tyrolean Lovers." *Godey's Lady's Book,* 20 (Feb., 1840), 77 - 80.

"Pride and Love." *Godey's Lady's Book,* 21 (Nov., 1840), 225 - 30.

"The Lover and the Poet." *Burton's Gentleman's Magazine,* 7 (Nov., 1840), 256 - 64.

"The Course of Love." *Godey's Lady's Book,* 22 (Mar., 1841), 128 - 33.

"The Head and the Heart." *Graham's Magazine,* 19 (July, 1841), 19 - 26.

"The Triumph of Love." *Godey's Lady's Book,* 24 (Mar., 1842), 158 - 65.

"The Masquerade." *Graham's Magazine,* 26 (Apr., 1845), 176 - 84.

2. Non-Fiction Books and Collections

Washington and the Generals of the American Revolution. Ed. R. W. Griswold. 2 vols. Philadelphia: Carey and Hart, 1847. Wallace is the author of the 96-page leading essay on Washington, which was reprinted, together with an essay by John M. Mackie, as *The Military and Civil Life of George Washington for the People.* Pamphlet. New York: William H. Graham, 1849.

Napoleon and the Marshals of the Empire. 2 vols. Philadelphia: Carey and Hart, 1848.

Can the Monopoly Lawfully be Abolished? Pamphlet. Burlington, N. J., 1849.

Art, Scenery and Philosophy in Europe. Philadelphia: Herman Hooker, 1855.

Literary Criticisms and Other Papers. Philadelphia: Parry and McMillan, 1856. Repr., Freeport, N.Y.: Books for Libraries Press, 1972.

Art and Scenery in Europe, With Other Papers. Philadelphia: Parry and McMillan, 1857.

Selected Fiction. Ed., George E. Hatvary. St. Paul, Minn.: John Colet
      Press. To appear in 1977 - 78.

3. Uncollected Essays and Articles
"Coleridge." *New York Mirror,* 13 (Dec. 5, 1835), 180 - 81.
"Washington Irving." *New York Mirror,* 13 (Dec. 19, 1835), 197.
"Dr. Channing." *New York Mirror,* 13 (Jan. 30, 1836), 245.
"Thomas Moore." *New York Mirror,* 13 (May 14, 1836), 365.
"Scraps from the Notebook of a Pedant." *New York Mirror,* 14 (Apr. 15,
      1837), 336.
"Sweepings from a Drawer." *Burton's Gentleman's Magazine,* 4 (Apr.,
      1839), 241 - 42; 5 (Aug., Nov., 1839), 96, 236.
"Mems for Memory." *Burton's Gentleman's Magazine,* 7 (Sept., Oct.,
      Nov., 1840), 151 - 52, 201 - 2, 249 - 50.
"Letter from Florence." *Home Journal,* 7 (Aug. 9, 1851).
"Letter from Florence." *Home Journal,* 7 (Oct. 4, 1851).
"Letter from Paris." *Home Journal,* 7 (Nov. 8, 1851).
"Biographical Sketch of the Hon. Wm. Bradford." *American Law Journal,*
      11 (Apr., 1852), 433 - 40.
"First Visit to Comte." *Home Journal,* 11 (Apr. 14, 1855).
"William Peter." *Home Journal,* 11 (May 12, 1855).
"Letter of a Persian Traveler . . ." *Home Journal,* 12 (Oct. 4, 1856).

4. Correspondence and Manuscripts
To William B. Wood, Apr. 27, 1851. *Home Journal,* 11 (Apr. 14, 1855).
To Emily C. Judson, Mar. 1, 1846. *Home Journal,* 12 (Mar. 8, 1856); repr.
      Kendrick (see below).
To Auguste Comte, June 23, 1851. August Comte. *Synthèse subjective.*
      Paris, 1856, I, liv; repr. Hawkins (see below).
Hatvary, George E. "The Wallace-Griswold Correspondence." *The Boston
      Public Library Quarterly,* 8 (Jan., 1956), 3 - 25.
Chief repositories of remaining manuscript letters: Historical Society of
      Pennsylvania. Massachusetts Historical Society. University of
      Virginia.

5. Appendix: Law Books
Smith, J. W. *A Selection of Leading Cases in Various Branches of the Law.*
      Ed. with J. I. Clark Hare. 2 vols. Philadelphia: T. and J. W. Johnson,
      1844.
Select Decisions of American Courts in Several Departments of the Law.
      With J. I. Clark Hare. 2 vols. Philadelphia: T. and J. W. Johnson,
      1847.
White, F. T. and O. D. Tudor. *A Selection of Leading Cases in Equity.*
      Ed. with J. I. Clark Hare. 2 vols. in 3. Philadelphia: T. and J. W.
      Johnson, 1849 - 51.
Meeson, R. and W. N. Welsby. *Reports of Cases Argued and Determined
      in the Courts of Exchequer and Exchequer Chamber . . . 1836 - 47.*

Ed. with J. I. Clark Hare. 16 vols. Philadelphia: T. and J. W. Johnson, 1845 - 49. (Wallace co-edited five additional sets of exchequer reports.)

SECONDARY SOURCES

The following abbreviations are used in this section:

ASPE - *Art, Scenery and Philosophy in Europe*
ASE - *Art and Scenery in Europe, with Other Papers*
LC - *Literary Criticisms and Other Papers*

ALLIBONE, SAMUEL A. *A Critical Dictionary of English Literature and British and American Authors Living and Deceased, from the Earliest Accounts to the Latter Half of the Nineteenth Century. . . .* 3 vols. Philadelphia: Lippincott, 1858 - 71. Important scholarly reference work of the period, giving Wallace a respectable place.

ANON. "Horace Binney Wallace." *Nassau Literary Magazine*, 19 (Oct., 1858), 66 - 72. Admires Wallace's mind, especially as evidenced in the posthumous volumes.

ANON. Review of *ASPE*. *New Englander*, 13 (May, 1855), 312 - 16. Disagrees with Wallace about the effect of the Reformation on art, but gives the work general praise.

ANON. Review of *ASPE* and *LC*. *Knickerbocker Magazine*, 48 (July, 1856), 76 - 79. Gives Wallace's discourse higher praise than his writings.

ANON. Review of *LC*. *Democratic Review*, 33 (May, 1856), 428 - 29. Places Wallace foremost among American critics.

ANON. Review of *Stanley*. *Burton's Gentleman's Magazine*, 4 (Jan., 1839), 65 - 66. Calls the novel, notwithstanding its faults, "the most forcible and original work of the day."

ANON. Review of *Stanley*. *Hesperian*, 2 (Mar., 1839), 409 - 10. Places the intellectual content above the narrative element, and gives an account of the novel's mysterious submission.

ANON. Review of *Stanley*. *New Yorker*, 6 (Dec. 22, 1838), 221. Calls it the most remarkable novel that has appeared in the century, but questions its readability, calling Tyler "an enormous failure."

ANON. Review of *Stanley*. *New York Review*, 4 (Jan., 1839), 237 - 39. Objects to the lack of artistic integration between the narrative and the dialogues, but regards the novel nevertheless as a work of genius.

BAYLESS, JOY. *Rufus Wilmot Griswold: Poe's Literary Executor*. Nashville, Tenn.: Vanderbilt University Press, 1943. Indispensable full-length study of Griswold; several references to Wallace.

BINNEY, HORACE. *Obituary*. Pamphlet. Philadelphia: Sherman, 1853); repr. *Home Journal*, 9 (Feb. 19, 1853); repr. *ASPE*, pp. xxiii-xxix. Eulogistic analysis of Wallace's mind and character by his uncle. In *ASPE*, followed by other obituaries (pp. xxix-xxxvi).

DUYCKINCK, E. A. and G. L. *Cyclopaedia of American Literature*. 2 vols. New York: Scribner, 1855. A major reference work of the period, giving Wallace a respectable place.

FISHER, SIDNEY GEORGE. Review of *ASPE*. *North American Review*, 81 (July, 1855), 212 - 44. Takes issue with Wallace's view of art as symbolical rather than imitative, but gives high praise amidst generous quotations.

GODWIN, PARKE. Review of *ASPE*. *Putnam's Monthly*, 6 (Sept., 1855), 267 - 76; repr. Godwin, *Out of the Past: Critical and Literary Papers*. New York: Putnam, 1870, pp. 302 - 25. Critical of Wallace's confining association of art with religion, but speaks highly of Wallace's powers. Reveals some details of his appearance and personality.

HATVARY, GEORGE E. "Horace Binney Wallace: A Study in Self-Destruction." *The Princeton University Library Chronicle*, 25 (Winter, 1964), 137 - 149. An exploratory article.

———. "Poe's Borrowings from H. B. Wallace." *American Literature*, 38 (Nov., 1966), 365 - 72. Presents parallel passages.

HAWKINS, RICHMOND L. *Auguste Comte and the United States (1816 - 1853)*. Cambridge: Harvard University Press, 1936. Important study of the subject, with appropriate references to Wallace.

HOWE, JULIA WARD. *Reminiscences, 1819 - 1899*. Boston and New York: Houghton, Mifflin, 1899. Gives a small but valuable glimpse into the author's friendship with Wallace from a perspective of nearly half a century.

KENDRICK, ASAHEL C. *The Life and Letters of Mrs. Emily C. Judson*. New York: Sheldon, 1860. Traces the friendship between Wallace and Emily Chubbuck through their correspondence.

PRITCHARD, JOHN P. *Criticism in America: An Account of the Development of Critical Techniques from the Early Period of the Republic to the Middle Years of the Twentieth Century*. Norman: University of Oklahoma Press, 1956. Several references to Wallace.

SPILLER, ROBERT E. "Horace Binney Wallace." *Dictionary of American Biography*. New York: Scribner, 1928 - 37. A good general recent account of Wallace's career.

WALLACE, JOHN WILLIAM. "Memoir." *ASPE*, pp. vii-xxi. An essentially fair, if somewhat eulogistic and reticent, account of Wallace's life by his brother. Quotes from Wallace's correspondence and remains a basic source for his life and career.

Index

(Wallace's works are listed under his name)

167

Saint Peter's University Library
Withdrawn